JATAKAS AND SIMILAR FABLES

JATAKAS AND SIMILAR FABLES

Jatakas and resembling Fables from other
famous ancient literatures

Key Words:
Select Jatakas and resembling Fables from Ramayana,
Mahabharata, Bhagabata, Kathasaritsagara, Hitopadesha,
Panchatantra, Odyssey, Arabian Nights and
Aesop's Fables. Forms of former births, Reigning Kings, Places Referred,
Repeated Titles, Stories Retold, Important Occasions.

Dr. Supriya Roy

MAHA BODHI BOOK AGENCY
4A, Bankim Chatterjee Street
Kolkata - 700 073, INDIA
2016

JATAKAS AND SIMILAR FABLES

By

Dr. Supriya Roy

First Published in 2016

Published by :
D.L.S. Jayawardana
MAHA BODHI BOOK AGENCY
4-A, Bankim Chatterjee Street, College Square
Kolkata-700 073 (India)
Phone : 9831077368, 98315 29452
Email : mahabodhibookagency@hotmail.com

Printed by :
Sagarika Press, Kolkata-700 009

ISBN : 978-93-84721-44-2

Price : ₹ 450.00

NAMO TASSA BHAGAVATO ARAHATO SAMMASAMBUDDHASSA

Dedicated to my Elder Brother
Dr Arnab Bandyopadhyay,
(A Renowned Psychiatrist & Book lover.)

PREFACE

While studying the Pali literature, the Jataka stories greatly fascinated me. Later on, I could realise that this vast composition consisting of 547 Tales is only a small portion of the Buddhist canonical literature. The more and more I read these; it appeared to be a massive collection of valuable treasures. In addition to its historic, literary, moral, social and religious values, it also encompasses many Fables/Stories, which are also available in the pre and post Buddha era literatures of India and abroad.

This interesting phenomenon attracted me to study the important compilations of indigenous as well as foreign origins. Since it is an endless subject in itself, a borderline had to be drawn carefully so that the study could be focussed on the relevant areas meaningfully. Accordingly, three each of pre and post Buddha indigenous compilations namely; the Ramayana, the Mahabharata, the Bhagabata, the Panchatantra, the Hitopadesa and the Kathasaritsagara were selected and studied. To ascertain the Jataka's relationship with the foreign literatures, three famous compilations, relating to the previous, contemporary and later periods have also been analysed. These are the Odyssey, the Aesop's Fables and the Arabian Nights.

This study itself is so massive, that I got the opportunity to keep myself fully immersed in it for about half a decade.

This book is based upon my research work titled, "Jatakas and the Contemporary Indian Fables" and shall provide the readers with many unknown and interesting facts. This would enable the readers not only to know further details about the Jataka, but also help them in further works/studies on the subject. For story lovers, they could derive the pleasure of reading the stories of the Jataka and of other world-class literatures side by side.

Happy reading!

Supriya Roy

ACKNOWLEDGEMENT

Any endeavour needs lots of active supports, helps and guidance in various forms from many persons around us. Writing this book is no exception to that rule. Without the whole hearted support of all, it would not have been possible to publish this book.

My family members and well-wishers have provided me their whole hearted supports, which enabled me to put my all out efforts behind this book.

My friends and teachers in the both Calcutta University and Jadavpur University have helped me a lot in my post-graduation and doctoral studies, which form the base for my writing this book. My heartfelt regards goes to Prof. (Dr) Manikuntala Halder (De) of Calcutta University for her consistent guidance.

Both the Supervisors of my Doctoral studies namely; Dr Sukomal Chaudhury and Dr Pradyot Kumar Datta have guided me to complete my study on the Jataka and other literatures.

I am extremely grateful to Dr Vandana Sinha, Director, Center for Art & Archaeology, American Institute of Indian Studies, India for kindly permitting me to reproduce the AIIS images in this book. All the Jataka images are obtained and reproduced through the kind courtesy of AIIS.

I express my sincere gratitude to all above and also to other persons, who have been the source of my inspiration, especially to Dr. Jagatpati Sarkar.

My sincere gratitude goes to the Publisher for his wholehearted support and cooperation.

I owe a lot to various libraries namely; the National Library - Kolkata, The Calcutta University Library, the Jadavpur University Library, the Sanskrit College Library, the Maha Bodhi Society Library, the Asiatic Society Library - Kolkata, the Asiatic Society Library - Mumbai, the Indian Museum Library - Kolkata and the Bombay Central Library, which provided me with valuable references and study materials.

I would also like to thank those in advance, who may like to share their valuable views on this book with me on; roykolkata7@gmail.com.

MAHAKAPI JATAKA

CONTENTS

1.0 ABOUT JATAKA

1.1 The Bodhisattva :

In the Buddhist literatures, Jataka refers to the stories of previous births of *Gautama Buddha.* According to the Buddhist belief, no one can become an enlightened one as *Buddha* in his very first birth itself. A person has to take hundreds of births in different forms, during which, he needs to practise ten model codes of conduct known as "Ten *Paramaits*" (e.g.; Charity, Conduct, Salvation, Vigour, Forgiveness, Amity, Truth, Thought, Inherence and Indifference).

Buddha had acquired the power of recollecting his previous births. On various occasions, he narrated the Jataka stories to his disciples and other persons in the form of *Gatahs* or verses. His listeners included his father, wife, warring groups of *Sakya* and *Kolio* etc., in addition to his regular disciples. Whenever any problem arose, Buddha used to recollect a similar story from one of his previous births and narrated the same to the people. Thereafter, he used to preach the righteous path to be followed. He also used to bring about an equation between the characters of the past story with the persons present.

1.2 Jataka in the Buddhist Canon :

The Buddhist canon is known as *Tipitaka* (Tri-*Pitaka* - or three baskets of knowledge). These are, *Vinaya Pitaka, Sutta Pitaka* and *Abhidhamma Pitaka.*

Vinaya Pitaka contains rules and regulations to be followed by the disciples and is divided into three parts.

Sutta Pitaka contains preliminary knowledge about the religion through prose, verse, tales, stories etc. It is divided into five *Nikayas* or volumes, e.g.; *Dirha Nikaya*, *Majjhima Nikaya*, *Samyukta Nikaya*, *Anguttara Nikaya* and *Khuddaka Nikaya*. While the first four *Nikayas* contain Lord *Buddha's* sermons and narrations, the fifth one is a collection of different books. *Jataka* is the tenth book of the *Khuddaka Nikaya*.

Abhidhamma Pitaka contains exposition of the religious theories enumerated in the *Sutta Pitaka*.

1.3 Navanga-Satthu-Sasana :

The *Tipitaka* again, comprise of nine types of narrations or '*Angas*', collectively called as "*Navanga - Satthu - Sasana*" consisting :

- *Sutta* - the teachings of Buddha compiled in prose.
- *Geyya* - Instructions in mixed prose and verse.
- *Veyyakarana* - Expositions & Commentaries.
- *Gataha* - Verses.
- *Udana* - Ecstatic utterances.
- *Itivuttaka* - Brief sayings.
- *Jataka* - Buddha's previous birth stories.
- *Abbhuta - dhamma* - Demonstration of supernatural powers.
- *Vedalla* - Preachings in the form of questions & answers.

The above-mentioned nine types are not nine divisions of the canon but are the classifications of the narrations.

1.4 Sections in Jataka tales :

A Jataka story in its present form is composed in prose and verse and comprises of three sections, viz;

1. *Pacchupannavatthu* (The present circumstances):

There always used to be an occasion in the *Sangha* or elsewhere, which led Lord Buddha to recollect a similar incident from one of his previous births. Such circumstances are narrated in this section in the form of prose or verse.

2. *Atitavatthu* (The story of former birth of Buddha recounted) :

This is the narration of story of Buddha's previous births in prose and verse.

3. *Samodhana* (Equating characters of present persons with past stories) :

This part is in prose, where Buddha identified the characters of the past story with the persons present at the time of story telling.

Gathas or verses were also a part of either past or present stories. *Gathas* made the Jataka more lively and interesting. *Gathas* are followed by *Veyyakarana* or short commentary, which explained the *Gathas* word for word.

1.5 Striking Resemblances :

It has been noticed that there are striking resemblances between many of the Jataka tales and the ancient Indian Fables of pre and post Buddha era. There are both similarities and disparities between the characters and stories of the Jatakas vis-a-vis other Fables.

Similarities and disparities are also noticeable between

the Jatakas and some renowned folk tales of foreign origin as well.

Such similar stories between the Jataka and other stories of the select Indian as well as foreign origin are brought forward side by side for interesting reading.

2.0 FOLK TALES AND THE JATAKA

2.1 Folk Tales :

Folk tales are the stories emanating in ancient times and continue to be told by the people generation after generations. The characters of the stories include, - besides human beings; animals, birds, trees, rivers, mountains and the likes.

Ancient people used to watch the behaviour of the nature, animals, birds and other creatures very closely. Resemblance of their humanlike behaviour tempted men to impose various imaginary characters in these and frame fictitious but interesting stories.

Subsequently, the characters of the stories have changed over periods. Ghosts, demons, gods etc. have made inroads into these tales. Gradually, the limbs of the body and other household articles etc. have found places in the diversified list of characters.

2.2 Style :

The Style of these tales included cooperation among various characters as well as human-like behaviours by them. Most of the stories were purely imaginary in nature. For example; a tiger wearing a bangle or a donkey wearing a lion's skin or an eagle demanding the flesh of a king etc. are purely imaginary in nature.

However, the authors could make the narrations so much interesting that the people loved these stories.

2.3 Form :

These tales survived through ages by means of oral communication as well as in the form of various books. The tales got modified while passing through different narrators and writers.

2.4 Folk Literature :

Folk tales form a principal part of the folk literature,

which also contains other works like poems verses, essays, history, paintings, sculptures etc.

2.5 Fables :

Fables are essentially the Folk Tales, which may contain a moral at the end. Whilst the main objective of the tales is to provide the readers/ listeners, the joy of reading / listening, the fables were used extensively to preach religious / social objectives. Through the fables, the people were taught to distinguish between good and bad in the best interest of the society and the mankind. We have observed the philosophers and the religious preachers using this route to enlighten the people in the most effective way.

2.6 Jataka - as Folk Literature :

Fables form a part of the contemporary literature. We observe that the Jataka not only served as a vehicle for propagation of Buddhism, but also has become an integral part of the ancient Indian/International literature. It is true that, some of these folk tales did exist in the pre-Jataka era. Still Jataka is the most comprehensive compilation of this part of the literature. It has a strong presence in the ancient Indian literature. These tales have not only been borrowed by the subsequent Indian literatures like *Panchatantra, Hitopodesa, Betal Panchavimsatika, Mangala Kavya, Katha-saritsagara*, etc. but also by the foreign literatures like, Aesop's fables, Arabian Nights, Gospel of Matthews, Plato's work, Caucer's Pandorer's tale and many others. The Jataka is a pure compilation of folk tales, written in a most simple language yet in most lucid and fascinating manner. This very style has made the Jataka nearer and dearer to all classes of people breaking the barrier of age, caste, creed and religion. The Jataka has ascended itself to the unbeatable top slot and could easily be termed as the "Gem" of folk literature.

3.0 JATAKA AND ANCIENT INDIAN LITERATURE

RAMA, LAKSHMANA, SITA AND HANUMAN

3.1 Jataka and the Ramayana

According to the tradition, the Ramayana came into being after the Vedas and the Upanisadas. The great epic was written by the renowned poet *Valmiki.* As per the legend, ascetic Valmiki expressed his deep grief in a prosodic structure in Sanskrit for the first time, when he witnessed a male stork being killed by a hunter while mating with his female companion.

"*Ma Nishada Pratisthang Tvamagamah Swasatih Samah*
Yath Crouncha-mithunadekambodhi Kamamohitam"

"Oh! Hunter, you won't ever earn esteem,-
Since you have killed a stork while mating"

The stanza or pair of line uttered by Valmiki is regarded as the first-ever poem or "*Sloka*"and the author came to be known as the *Adi-Kavi* or the ancient-most poet. Ramayana was said to have been composed by him much before the birth of the Buddha and was regarded as the oldest epic of India. The time frame of compiling the Ramayana at least dates back to 1500 BC. We observe that some of the Jatakas contain stories from the Ramayana in some form or the other. In this chapter such exclusive stories are presented.

3.1.1 Devadharma Jataka *(Devadhamma Jātaka - 6)*

Once upon a time, a king named Brahmadatta reigned in the kingdom of Benares. Bodhisattva had born to the queen of king Brahmadatta. He was named as prince Mahimsasa. When he was about three years old, his brother prince Moon had born. By the time Moon could run around, their mother died. The king married another lady, to whom prince Sun had born. The overjoyed king promised to bestow a boon to the new queen at a later date.

When prince Sun grew up, the queen asked for the boon from the king. She wanted that her son Sun, though youngest, be announced as the Crown Prince superceding the king's two existing elder sons. Since, this was contrary to the rules of the society that only the eldest son would be the natural choice for the Crown Prince, the king declined to accept this. He tried to persuade the queen in vain.

The king, sensing evil intentions of the stepmother, asked both the elder princes to go to the forest to live incognito for 12 years and to return and ascend the throne thereafter upon his death.

Actually, all the three brothers had great love, affection and esteem for each other. When princes Mahimsasa and Moon prepared to go the forest, prince Sun also joined them. He could not be desisted by others.

When the three brothers reached the Himalayan region, Mahimsasa asked the youngest brother Sun to go to the nearby pool to fetch some drinking water. Accordingly, he proceeded to a nearby pool. A water-sprite lived in that pool. As soon as Sun stepped into the pool, he was seized by the water sprite, which asked him the meaning of "Virtue". Sun failed to give satisfactory reply and was held in captivity by the sprite. Since he did not return within a reasonable period, his elder Moon came in search of him. He also fell in the trap and was held captive by the sprite. Finally, Prince Mahimsasa came and could give the proper reply to the sprite's questions. The sprite was happy at this and offered to free one brother. Mahimsasa opted for the youngest, being the son of the stepmother. The sprite was happy with his wisdom and freed both the brothers. They spent the entire period in the forest under the good care of the sprite. Later, on the king's death, they returned to

Benares along-with the water sprite. Prince Mahimsasa ascended to the throne. He designated prince Moon his Viceroy and prince Sun the Commander-in-Chief.

As in the Ramayana, in the olden days, Dasaratha was the king of Ayodhya. He was married to three queens, Kaushalya, Kaikeyee and Sumitra. Four sons were born out of these three queens. Rama was the eldest son born to Kaushalya. Bharata was second one born to Kaykeyee. Sumitra had two younger sons named Lakshman and satrughan. Once king Dasaratha went for hunting and returned in a badly injured condition. Kaikeyee nursed him devotedly and cured him. Pleased Dasaratha wanted to bestow her with two boons. Kaikeyee said she wished to pray for it at an appropriate time. When Rama became matured, the king arranged for his coronation as the Crown Prince. On the day of coronation, Kaikeyee reminded the king about the two promised boons. The timing of asking for the boon surprised the king. The queen asked for two boons; 14 years' exile to the forest for Rama and Kingdom for her son Bharata, who was younger to Rama. Dasaratha got the worst shock of his life. He declined to give in to the queen's heinous wishes. Rama convinced his father that it was his duty to keep up his father's promise, may what came. He prepared to go to the forest. Rama got wed to Sita only in the recent past. She expressed her determination to follow the footsteps of her husband at any cost. Lakshman's whole world revolved around his eldest brother Rama and as such nobody was able to dissuade him from accompanying Rama. Ultimately, Rama went to the forest alongwith his wife Sita and brother Lakshman. Dasaratha was unable to bear the pain of Rama's departure and died. Bharata was kept away to his maternal uncle's place. When he came to know about this development, he rushed to get back Rama. On the advice of Rama, he went back to

Ayodhya with the slippers of Rama and ruled the kingdom in the name of Rama.

This Jataka story is a combination of both the Ramayana and the Mahabharata. The Crown Prince and his brother's going to the forest at the instance of the stepmother is similar to the Ramayana. The stepbrother's accompanying the Crown Prince to the forest and the latter's showing more affection to the former in the Jataka is an exemplary teaching of Buddhism.

The Jataka story imparts the great philosophy of shunning hatred and bringing peace to the mankind even at the cost of great sufferings.

3.1.2 Dasaratha Jataka *(Dasaratha Jātaka - 461)*

As per this Jataka, king Dasaratha reigned in Benares righteously and had sixteen thousand wives. His Queen-consort gave births to two sons named Rama Pandita (Rama) and Lakshana and a daughter named Sita. In due course, when the queen consort died, the king married another lady. The new queen gave birth to prince Bharata. The king, being overwhelmed with joy, promised to bestow a boon to her.

When Bhrata was seven years old, the queen asked the king for the promised boon that, Bharata be declared the crown prince. The king grew angry at this but could not deter the queen from her demand.

The king consulted the soothsayers, who predicted that the king would die after 12 years. Lest the stepmother harmed his elder sons, the king called the elder sons and asked them to spend 12 years in the forest and then return to ascend the throne upon his death.

While Rama and Lakshana prepared to go the forest,

their sister Sita also joined them. They went to the Himalayas and lived in a hermitage on fruits brought by Sita and Lakshana.

The king died after nine years but the courtiers did not allow Bharata to be the king. Bharata, along-with the courtiers came to Rama's hermitage and informed about his father's death. Rama, aware of the theory of "Impermanence of beings", remained unmoved by the shocking news of the demise of his beloved father. When Lakshana and Sita returned after fetching fruits, Rama ordered them to stand in the water of a pool to avoid shock and then disclosed the sad news. Both Lakshana and Sita fainted thrice in the pool. Rama remained steady and explained the "Theory of Impermanence" to all present.

Bharata and the courtiers requested Rama to go back to Benares and take charge of the kingdom. Rama said that he would return only after 12 years as desired by his father but sent Lakshana and Sita with Bharata.

Bharta carried Rama's wooden slippers to Benares and placed those on the throne. The slippers ruled the kingdom for 3 years. Whenever a case was adjudged wrongly the slippers used to beat upon each other and on right judgment, those remained unmoved.

Rama returned after three more years and ascended the throne with great pomp. He wedded his sister Sita and made her Queen-consort.

In the Ramayana, king Dasharatha had a fourth son named Satrughna. Sita was not Rama's sister; she was Rama's wife and king Janaka's foster-daughter. Rama, Lakshana and Sita went to the forest for 14 years and fought with various evils including Ravana, who abducted Sita. Ramayana does not mention about Rama's announcing father's death news to Lakshana and Sita keeping them in water. Rather, as per the Ramayana, Rama got fainted on haring the news of his father's sad demise and was deeply immersed in grief.

Here, we observe that the Dasharatha Jataka has more resemblances with the Ramayana than the Devadharma Jataka (6). As per the practice of the time of Ramayanà, marrying own sister was not permitted. But as per Sakya culture, this was an acceptable norm and widely practised.

In Devadharma Jataka, pseudonyms were used. It is very clear that although the Ramyana has been used as the basic source in both the Jatakas, names, incidents and stories have been altered to suit the need for preaching human values.

3.1.3 Jayadwisha Jataka *(Jayaddisa Jātaka - 513)*

As per Jayadwisha Jataka, an Ogress (a female Yaksha) carried away a royal infant and reared him as her own son. The boy grew up with his mother and turned into a man-eater (Yaksha). He dwelt in the forest. Incidentally, one day he caught his own royal brother without knowing his identity and wanted to have a meal out of him. The royal brother told the Yaksha that he would be back after fulfilling a promise he made to a Brahmin. The Yaksha set him free to return as his meal after redeeming his promises to a Brahmin. Bodhisattva had born as the son of this king. He convinced his father that he would be able to tackle the issue and return alive. The father, though unwilling, had to allow his son to go. Bodhisattva went to the forest and surrendered to the man-eater as a victim in his father's stead. The prince recognized the man-eater as his uncle and converted him into an ascetic.

Here, the forest, in which the man-eater dwelt, is named

as Dandaka forest and the prince is referred to as Rama. We get the names of Rama and the Dandaka forest in the Ramayana. There are no other similarities with the Ramayana.

3.1.4 Sarabhanga Jataka *(Sarabhañga Jātaka - 522)*

An archer displayed wonderful skills in archery. He declined the honour and wealth bestowed upon him by the king. He retired as an ascetic. He built a hermitage on the bank of river Godavari. He came to be known as Sarabhanga Muni (ascetic). A host of disciples gathered around him. One of his great pupils named Kisavachha took abode in Kumbhavati in a province of the kingdom of king Dandaki. He suffered great humiliation in the hands of the people of Kumbhavati and king Dandaki himself. As a result, the kingdom of king Dandaki perished with all its population and came to be known as dreaded Dandaka forest (*Dandakarnya*). Later, three kings and the god king Indra came to the hermitage of Sarabhanga and asked him a few questions. Upon getting proper replies, they went back.

In the Ramayana, the background of Sarabhanga is not mentioned but he is described as one of the greatest ascetic of that time. Rama with Lakshana and Sita went to his hermitage. They found god-king Indra discussing with the ascetic. In Rama's presence Sarabhanga died and his soul went to the heaven. The story of formation of Dandaka forest also differs with the Ramayana.

As per the Ramayana, king Danda got highly attracted to his chief priest Sukracharyya's daughter Araja and had sex with her without obtaining prior consent from her father. When Sukracharyya came to know about this, he got furious. As per Sukracharyya's curse, the place with its inhabitants got destroyed in seven days and got converted into a dreaded forest. The forest came to be known as Dandaka forest.

3.1.5 Alambusha Jataka *(Alambusa Jātaka - 523)*

In Alambusha Jataka, an ascetic resided in a hermitage in a forest. One day, he sighted a beautiful nymph and discharged semen on the grass in a field adjoining his hermitage. A doe, while grazing in the field, ate his semen mixed with grass and gave birth to a deerlike human boy. The hermit reared the boy and named him Rishishringa. The boy became an ascetic and his holiness excited the jealousy of god Indra, who sent a heavenly nymph by name Alambusha to seduce him. She did her job well and kept Rishishringa immersed in sensual pleasure for long three years. Thereafter, Rishishringa realized his mistake and restored to his previous holy life leaving Alambusha.

3.1.6 Nalinika Jataka *(Nalinikā Jataka - 526)*

In this Jataka, the birth story of Rishishringa has been narrated as in the Alambusha Jataka. The holiness of Rishishringa bothered god Indra, who hit upon a plan to dessuade him from virtuous path. There were draught in the kingdom of Kashi for three consecutive years, bringing in famine and severe sufferings to its inhabitants. On the advice of Indra, the king sent his daughter Nalinika to seduce the ascetic. Nalinika performed her assigned task well and came back. As a result, rainfall resumed and the country was restored to normalcy. Rishishringa realized his mistake and resumed his meditation.

In the Ramayana, a saint named Bibhandaka used to reside in a hermitage in a forest. One day he saw a heavenly nymph named Urvashi to pass by. The saint was so much attracted to her beauty that he could not control himself. He discharged semen and washed himself in the adjoining 'Great Lake'. A doe came to the lake for drinking water. It took the water mixed with semen and became pregnant. In due course of time, it gave birth to a human-like baby which had a horn on its head. Bibhandaka kept the boy in his hermitage and grew him up as a saint. The boy was named as Rishyashringa, which literally means a saint (Rishi) having horn (Shringa). The kingdom of Anga was experiencing draught and severe famine because of unjust rules of its king Lompada. When he asked the priests about the remedy, they advised him to get saint Rishyashringa in his kingdom. Here, the ascetic was seduced by a group of prostitutes, deputed by the king Lompada. They lured Rishishringa to the palace of the king. The king welcomed him and gave in his daughter Shanta married to him. Rain resumed and normalcy restored. Rishishringa continued to stay in the Anga kingdom alongwith his wife.

Dasharatha, the king of Ayodhya did not have any issue. He was keen to have a few. He performed Asvamedha yagna. As per advice of his charioteer Sumantra, he brought Rishishringa and his wife to his kingdom from Anga to perform the rituals of the yagna. He performed the yagna and stayed there for a year. The three queens of king Dasaratha delivered four sons in due course.

It is evident that both the Jataka stories have their roots in the Ramayana, which have been altered marginally.

3.1.7 Shyama Jataka *(Sāma Jātaka - 540)*

In Shyama Jataka, a hunter's son married another hunter's daughter but both became ascetics and lead pious lives in a hermitage in the Himalayan forest. On the advice of god Indra, the wife gave birth to a son without mating. When the boy grew up, an angry snake blinded the parents. The boy looked after the blind parents.

One day, the king of Benares, named Piliyayaksha, came to the forest for hunting. Seeing the boy collecting water from the river Mrigasammata, he wilfully shot an arrow to kill him. The arrow pierced the body of the boy from right to left and he collapsed there. Upon learning his dutiful affection towards his parents, the king repented for his misdeed. He took the pitcher and the body of the boy to the hermitage and confessed to his sins to the parents. Even after knowing the heineous crime committed by the king, the parents did not curse or utter any harsh words to him. Rather, they offered him respectful hospitality. Due to such heavenly virtue of the parents, the boy recovered fully and the parents regained their eyesight.

As in the Ramayana, king Dasharatha went to the jungle for hunting. In a pitch-dark night, he heard some sound, which was alike the sound made by an elephant. It was actually the sound of filling pitcher with water from river. An elderly blind ascetic couple lived in a nearby hermitage. It was their only son, who came to river bank to fetch water for them. The king was proficient in hitting a target by releasing an arrow tracking a sound. The king did no mistake in this case too. His arrow pierced the heart of the boy. When the proud king reached the spot, he was taken aback at his own cruel deeds. He went to the hermitage, narrated the parents about the accident and brought them to the spot. The parents could not bear the shock an died by the fire of the pyre of their beloved son. Before dying, they cursed that the king would also have to die from a similar shock.

In this case, the story of the Ramyana had been modified in the Jataka to accommodate the Buddhist philosophy of refraining from having hatred even towards the worst enemy. This has transformed the sinners to become benefactors to the mankind. Additionally, the parents, by their virtue, not only could revive their otherwise dead son, but also regained their lost eyesight.

From the foregoing we observe that;

➭ The Ramayana is a well-knit epic composed in a logical and sequential manner without leaving any scope for any contradiction among its various events / stories.

➭ Jataka is a compilation of different and individualistic stories without having any correlation among them. On the contrary, there are significant variations among several Jataka stories themselves while narrating the same events / stories.

➭ The aforesaid Jataka stories seem to have emanated from the Ramayana and have been reproduced after incorporating some minor changes.

IN THE BATTLE FIELD OF KURUKSHETRA

3.2 Jatakas and the Mahabharata

The Mahabharata is regarded as the epic composed after the Ramayana around the 1000 BC. The Mahabharata is traditionally known to have been authored by the famous saint Vedavyas and written by Lord Ganesha himself. There are traditional and logical links between the two Epics. In the Mahabharata, some stories/incidents of the Ramayana have been referred to without bringing in any contradictions. In fact, king Dasharatha of the Ramayana hails from the Ikshaku family. Koravas and Pandavas of the Mahabharata are descendants of king Bharata, the son of king Dyushyanta and Shakuntala. Lord Buddha's clan 'Sakyas' said to have been evolved from Ikshaku hereditary, which came into being post Mahabharata war. The references of the Ramayana in the Mahabharata clearly determine the precedence list. We now proceed to reading those Jatakas, alongwith their counterparts in the Mahabharata.

3.2.1 Devadharma Jataka *(Devadhamma Jataka - 6)*

Once upon a time, a king named Brahmadatta reigned in the kingdom of Benares. Bodhisattva had born to the queen of king Brahmadatta. He was named as prince Mahimsasa. When he was about three years old, his brother prince Moon had born. By the time Moon could run around, their mother died. The king married another lady, to whom prince Sun had born. The overjoyed king promised to bestow a boon to the new queen at a later date.

When prince Sun grew up, the queen asked for the boon from the king. She wanted that her son Sun, though youngest, be announced as the Crown Prince superceding the king's two existing elder sons. Since, this was contrary to the rules of the society that only the elder son would be the natural choice for the Crown Prince, the king declined to accept this. He tried to persuade the queen in vain.

The king, sensing evil intentions of the stepmother, asked both the elder princes to go to the forest to live incognito for 12 years and to return and ascend the throne thereafter upon his death.

Actually, all the three brothers shared great love, affection and esteem for each other. When princes Mahimsasa and Moon prepared to go the forest, prince Sun also joined them. He could not be desisted by any one.

When the three brothers reached the Himalayan region, Mahimsasa asked the youngest brother Sun to go to the nearby pool to fetch some drinking water. Accordingly, he proceeded to a nearby pool. A water-sprite lived in that pool. As soon as Sun stepped into the pool, he was seized by the water sprite, which asked him the meaning of "Virtue". Sun failed to give satisfactory reply and was held in captivity by the sprite. Since he did not return within a reasonable period, his elder Moon came in search of him. He also fell in the trap and was held captive by the sprite. Finally, Prince Mahimsasa came and could give the proper replies reply to the sprite's questions. The sprite was happy at this and offered to free one brother. Mahimsasa opted for the youngest, being the son of the stepmother. The sprite was happy with his wisdom and freed both the brothers. They spend the entire period in the forest under the good care of the sprite. Later, on the king's death, they returned to Benares along-with the water sprite. Prince Mahimsasa ascended to the throne. He designated prince Moon his Viceroy and prince Sun the Commander-in-Chief.

In the story of the Mahabharata, Dhritarashtra and Pandu were two brothers. Since the Elder brother Dhritarashtra was blind from the birth, Pandu became the king as per the rules prevailing at that time. Dhritarashtra had one hundred sons and a daughter from his wife Gandhari. They came to be known as Koravas. Pandu had five sons from his two wives, who were called the Pandavas. After the death of Pandu, the senior-most Pandava; Yudhisthira ascended the throne. The eldest Korava brother Duryodhana did not like this and wanted to be the king himself. In order to fulfil his ambition, he played tricks one after the other. He invited the Pandavas to play dice with him. Pandavas got defeated by the Koravas in a deceiving game. As per the precondition of this game, they accepted to live in exile in the forest for twelve years and spend one-year in incognito. Accordingly, they went to live in the forest alongwith their mother Kunti and common wife Draupadi. Towards the end of the twelfth year, one day they felt very thirsty after chasing a deer in the deep forest. Yudhisthira asked brother Nakula to fetch some water from a nearby pond. There, Nakula was asked by a Yaksha guarding the pond, to reply to his questions before taking the water. He ignored the Yaksha's order and lay dead on the bank. Subsequently, the other brothers Sahadeva, Arjuna and Bhima also met same fate. Finally, Yudhisthira came and patiently replied to all questions asked by the Yaksha. Being pleased, the Yaksha wanted to set to life one of the brothers. Yudhisthira asked for the life of his stepbrother Nakula. He clarified that since Nakula was his step-brother, it would be right for him to ask for his life. The Yaksha, being extremely happy with his wisdom brought all brothers to life and also awarded three boons. He then revealed his real identity as Dharma (the god of 'Religion'), who came in the disguise of Yaksha.

Thus, we observe that, whilst the first part of the story corroborates with the Ramayana, its later part is almost a shadow of the story in the Mahabharata.

3.2.2 Kastha-hari Jataka *(Kaṭṭhāhaṛi Jātaka - 7)*

A king, while roaming in the garden fell in love with a wood-picker girl. He had intimate relations with her and made her pregnant. He presented his Signet ring to her and said that, if she bore a daughter, she should sell the ring to rear up her. In case she gave birth to a boy, she should come back to the king along with the boy and the ring. In due course, she delivered a boy. When the boy grew up a little, she took him to the court of the king. The king refused to recognize the lady and the Signet ring. He also denied having any affair with the lady. The lady threw the boy up in air saying that, if he were really the king's son, he would remain in the mid air or else, he would fall on the ground and die. The child remained steady in the mid air and declared that he was the king's son. At this, the king accepted the boy as his own son and accepted the lady as his Queen-consort.

As per the Mahabharata, Saint Viswamitra started extreme meditation. In order to dissuade him from the meditation, god king Indra sent an extremely beautiful nymph named Menaka from the heaven. Menaka could seduce Viswamitra and had sex with him. She remained there for about a year and kept Viswamitra fully immersed in sensual pleasure. In due course, a girl child was born to Menaka. Menaka abondened her in the forest and went back to the heaven. Viswamitra again resumed his meditation afresh. The abandoned infant was detected by a vulture (*Sakuna*). The vulture and its companions formed an umbrella over the baby to protect it. Saint Kanva, who lived in the nearby hermitage, discovered the infant protected by vultures (*Sakuna*). He took her to his abode and reared her as her own daughter. She was named Sakuntala. She gradually grew up to a beautiful young lady.

Duyshanta was a great king at that time. One day, he set out with his men for hunting in the jungle. After a great deal of hunting, he was alone and chanced to visit the hermitage of saint Kanva. He met the beautiful Sakuntala there. He, at once fell in love with her and married her as per the Gandharva rules and had physical union with her. The king assured her that he would return to take her to his palace. In due course a boy named Bharata was born to Sakuntala. When he grew up, Sakuntala took him to the king. The king felt embarrassed to accept the facts in his court in the presence of all others. He feigned ignorance about the relationship he had with her. There came an oracle from the heaven declaring that the boy was the king's son. Thereupon, the king had no choice but to accept his wife and son. The son was made the Crown Prince. In due course, Bharata became a great king. This Jataka story is also based on the Mahabharata and reproduced with minor modifications.

3.2.3 Mitachinti Jataka *(Mitacinti Jātaka - 114)*

Once upon a time, there lived three fishes in the river of Benares. They were named Bahuchinti (over-thoughtful), Alphachinti (less-thoughtful) and Mitachinti (proper-thoughtful). Earlier, they had been living in the jungle areas, where, no fishermen ventured. Now they came near the human infested town, where, chances of getting caught in the net were significant. Mitachinti cautioned his friends about the impeding danger and requested them to go elsewhere. But the other two were enjoying stay over there since they were getting better food and were reluctant to move out. One day, foolish Bahuchinti and Alpachinti were moving forward faster to grab foods, if there were any. They did not pay any heed to look around carefully if there were any danger. They even failed to notice the net cast by the fishermen. As a result, they got trapped in the fishermen's net. Seeing this, Mitachinti played a trick. He jumped in the water just before and also after the net in such a way that the fishermen got illusioned to think that the net got torn from both sides. They lifted the net from front and the back side. The fishes took this opportunity to swim away fast to safety.

As per the Mahabharata, three fishes lived in a pond. Their names were, Anagata Bidhata (foresighted), Pratyutpannamati (intelligent) and Dirgha-Sutra (slow-going). One day, the fishermen started dewatering the pond. Anagata Bidhata cautioned the two friends and said, "Let us go out now, or else, we will be trapped". Pratyutpannamati said, "Don't worry, I shall find a way out at the nick of the moment." Dirgha-Sutra opined "We need not hurry about anything now". Anagata Bidhata swam to safety to another reservoir. When the water in the pond receded, the fishermen caught all the fishes and passed a rope through their mouths like a garland. Pratyutpannamati bit the rope strongly pretending that he too had been tied in the rope. Then the fishermen took the garland of fishes to a big reservoir for washing. Pratyutpannamati escaped to safety. Dirgha-Sutra could not go anywhere and was killed.

The Jataka story is a slight variation to the story in the Mahabharata.

3.2.4 Birala Jataka *(Bilāra Jātaka - 128)*

In this Jataka, Bodhisattva had born as the leader of hundreds of rats. The rats went in a troop every morning is search of food and returned in the evening together. A jackal hit upon a plan to eat the rats. One morning, he took position near the rats' den and stood on one leg facing the Sun. He kept his mouth opened and kept on snuffing air. When asked by the leader of the rats, he explained that he was looking towards the Sun to worship him, standing on one leg to reduce his burden on the earth and was inhaling air, since this was his only food from that day. Mistaking him to be of saintly natured they believed him and did not consider him an enemy. From next day onwards the jackal used to stand the same way but used to catch the hindmost rat and devour him. The count of the rats gradually dwindled. Doubting the jackal's saintliness, one day Bodhisattva remained on the hindmost of the troop. The jackal as usual pounced on him and tried to devour him. As planned, Bodhisattva, along with other rats attacked the jackal and killed him.

3.2.5 Agnika Jataka *(Aggika Jātaka - 129)*

In this Jataka also, Bodhisattva had born as a king of a group of rats. A jackal, which was trapped in a jungle fire, lost all hair on his body in the flame leaving only a tuft of hair on his crown. With this, he looked similar to a Brahmin pundit, who used to sport a similar hair style. He looked different than other jackals and used this as an opportunity to to fool the rats. He offered his services as a supervisor to the rat brethren. The rats, taking him for a saint agreed to this. The jackal used to devour the hind-most rat as detailed in the previous Jataka. Discovering this, the rat-king Bodhisattva drove him away.

As per the Mahabharata, a cat hit upon a plan to befool the rats. He sat with his both hands folded up and declared that he had become a saint and have stopped killing of rats and birds. The rats, believing this, made him their friend and used to take him along with them while going to river and returning. The cat used to kill and eat the hind-most rat everyday and the population of the rats started diminishing. A rat named Dindika volunteered to stay in the hind-most position to unravel the truth. He was killed and eaten by the cat. Rats understood the untold story with the vanishing of Dindika and left the company of the cat immediately.

Both the above-mentioned Jataka stories are similar to the story of the Mahabharata. The 'Cat' in the Mahabharata has become 'Jackal' in the Jatakas. The name of the Jataka No. 128 is 'Birala' Jataka, meaning "Cat", although a 'Jackal' has been portrayed as the villain of the story.

3.2.6 Rajavibada Jataka *(Rājovāda Jātaka - 151)*

In this Jataka, Bodhisattva was the king of Benares and he used to rule his kingdom with great wisdom and justice. Everyone in the country used to praise his righteous rule. One day, when he was travelling in his chariot through a narrow road, Mallika, the king of Kosala came in his chariot from the opposite side. Drivers of both the chariots decided that the superior king's chariot should be given way first. Since both the kings were equal in age, power, wealth, glory, size of kingdom etc., they decided to measure the superiority with respect to the virtues of the kings. Both the drivers started describing the virtues of their masters one by one. While the king of Kosala adopted a tit for tat policy to resolve each issue, the king of Benares adopted polite way to resolve each case. Hence the king of Benares was adjudged superior and was given way first.

Mahabharata's story relates to Suhotra, the king of Kuru and king Sibi of Usinara. One day, both the kings came face to face while travelling in their respective chariots. Both the kings were almost equal in their ages, wealth and wishdom. They greeted each other. But they were unable to decide as to who was superior between them. As per the existing rules, the right of way was to be given to the superior. At that time, saint Narada appeared at that spot. He was requested by both to adjudge the superiority between the two kings. Narada declared king Sibi superior to king Suhotra. Accordingly, king Sibi was given way first. The Jataka story is the replica of the Mahabharata except for the fact that in the later case, saint Narada adjudged the superiority in favour of king Sibi.

3.2.7 Sila-mimansa Jataka *(Sīlavīmamsa Jātaka - 330)*

In this Jataka, Bodhisattva was a courtier to a king. He wanted to test the power of virtue. He stole a coin from the king's treasury on each of the three consecutive days. He was caught and brought before the king and pronounced a thief. He took the permission of the king to lead an ascetic's life. On his way to the Himalayas, he observed that a bird stole a piece of meat from a stall and flew away. The bird was attacked by the other birds for the piece of meat. They tried to snatch away the piece of meat and hit him with their beaks, claws and nails. As soon as the bird left the piece of meat, the attacks stopped. Another bird, which seized the piece of meat, became the new target of the other birds. Bodhisattva realized that having desires was like inviting sorrow. Getting rid of desires begot him peace.

Bodhisattva had another observation. A maid named Pingala waited anxiously till midnight for her lover. The lover did not turn up even after long wait. Pingala finally lost hope of meeting the lover and abandoned longing for him. This brought peace of mind for her and she could go to sleep peacefully thereafter. This was another eye-opener for Bodhisattva. He could realise that thirst for lust was another reason for embracing sorrow. Getting rid of this vice begets happiness. With firm determination, he stepped forward towards his destiny as an ascetic.

The Mahabharata, exactly same stories as the preceeding ones of the bird and Pingala appear. Hence, the stories of the Mahabharata and the Jataka are one and the same.

3.2.8 Kuntani Jataka *(Kunṭani Jātaka - 343)*

In this, Bodhisattva was the virtuous ruler of Benares. He had two baby boys. He had a bird, which used to carry messages to distant places. The bird also had two chicks. One day, when the bird was away on duty, the king's sons squeezed the chicks to death. The bird, on return heard the death news. She, on getting opportunity, drove the royal boys in a tiger's cage, which killed them. The bird narrated this to the king and said that she was leaving the palace. The king said that the bird had already taken the justified revenge could now stay back peacefully. The bird said, it would be unwise to continue to stay in the enemy's den and flew away to safety.

In the Mahabharata, both the bird and the king had one offspring each. The prince was a kid. He killed the chick by throttling its neck. At the time of the incident, the bird was away. In this case, the bird took her revenge by blinding the king's son with her beaks. The king took this sportingly and told the bird that she has taken rightful revenge by blinding the prince. In this story also, the bird refused to the king's proposal to stay back. She flew away feeling that the place was no longer safe for her. Name of the bird in the Mahabharata is Pujani.

3.2.9 Sutanu Jataka *(Sutano Jātaka - 398)*

Brahmadatta, the king of Benares once went to a forest for hunting. A Yaksha named Makhadeva caught the king.

He wished to kill the king and eat him. To protect himself from getting killed, the king promised to send him a person everyday along with rice, so that the Yaksha could eat both the man and the rice. Initially, the king sent all prisoners as Yaksha's food. Afterwards, nobody else was available for this purpose. The king proclaimed to award one thousand gold coins to any person, who was ready to go to the Yaksha as his meal. Bodhisattva had born in a poor family and was named Sutanu (well-built). He agreed to go to the Yaksha as his food for the earning.

Before proceeding, he took the king's golden shoes, golden umbrella and best quality rice cooked with meat in a big golden bowl. He met the Yaksha and told him that, in case he wanted uninterrupted supply of such good food, he should leave killing men. This will also help him in having a better birth next time. The Yaksha agreed and came along with him to the kingdom. The Yaksha was settled by the king on the outskirts of the kingdom and was served good food regularly. The Yaksha stopped eating human beings. The king was happy and appointed Bodhisattva the Commander-in-Chief of his army.

As per the Mahabharata, Pandavas were then roaming in the forest. They were residing with a Brahmin family for a few days in the town of "Eka-Chakra". One day, they heard the wailing of the family members. On enquiry, it could be gathered that, one of them have to go and sacrifice himself as meal to a demon named Vaka. On hearing this, the second Pandava, Bhima volunteered to go to the Vaka with food. He went there at the hour of appointment and started eating the food himself, which was sent for Vaka. Seeing this, Vaka got furious and tried to kill Bhima. But Bhima overpowered and killed Vaka. His bravery saved the inhabitant of that place from the man-eater.

The Jataka story is a shadow of the story of the Mahabharata. Since Bhima had a great physique, he used to be called *'Sutanu'* or 'Well-built'.

3.2.10 Maha-suka Jataka *(Mahāsuka Jātaka - 429)* Kshudra-suka Jataka *(Cullasuka Jātaka - 430)*

Once upon a time Bodhisattva had born as a Parrot-king and dwelt in a grove of a fig tree in the Himalayas on the bank of the river Ganges. He was very pious and lived there happy and contented. God-king Indra *(Sakka)* wanted to test his virtue and he withered up the tree, which became a mere stump perforated with holes. The parrot king did not leave the tree. He ate the dust of the tree and drank the water of the Ganges and perched atop the stump to withstand the wrath of the wind and the Sun. Indra, being astonished, came to him in the form of a royal Goose preceded by his wife Suja. On his query, the Parrot-king said that, the Fig tree had reared him from the childhood. He asserted Indra that he was not going to leave the tree in its distress. Hearing this, Indra praised the Parrot-king and rejuvenated the tree with beautiful branches, green leaves and tasty fruits.

The story of the Mahabharata narrates that a pious parrot dwelt in a tree in a forest. One day a hunter released a poisoned arrow to kill a deer. The arrow missed its target and hit the tree. Being struck by the poisonous arrow, the tree started withering. But the parrot did not leave the distressed tree. The God-king Indra came to the parrot in the disguise of a Brahmin and asked the parrot the reasons for staying in the dying tree. The parrot could recognize him as Indra and said that he was grateful to the tree since it had reared him up and that he could not leave it under any circumstances. Indra was happy and he rejuvenated the tree.

Both the stories are one and the same.

3.2.11 Krishna-dwipayana Jataka (*Kaṇhadīpāyana Jātaka* - 444)

In ancient days, there lived two Brahmin friends in a certain village. They possessed immense wealth. Still they felt that living, as ascetics would be better than living as householders. They left behind their houses and took up living as ascetics and started staying in the Himalayas. After 50 years they came back to their town. One of them, named Mandavya started meditating in the cemetery, whilst the other named Dwipayana dwelt with another friend, also named Mandavya. One day a few thieves stole valuable from the town. On being chased by the security, they dumped the booty near the door of saint Mandavya's hut and hid in its premises. The securities reached there in a short while and enquired with Mandavya about the thieves. As Mandavya was in deep meditation, he was not aware of the incidents and could not answer them. The thieves and the booty were recovered from the premises. Saint Mandavya was mistaken for the leader of the thieves. The king ordered him to be impaled on a stake. Mandavya did not die and he continued with the meditation in the impaled condition. Through meditation he could recall that he had pierced a fly in his early childhood in his former birth. Because of that he got such punishment at a later age. He continued to live in that condition. One day Dwipayana came and found him in that state. He sat below him. Blood from Mandavya's body came down and got sprayed all over his body. His skin got darkened with the dried blood and he came to be known as Krishna (Black) Dwipayana. The king came later and understood his mistake. But the stake could not be removed from the body of Mandavya and the portion protruding outside his body was cut. He lived with the peg inserted in his body. Black Dwipayana went back to the householder Mandavya. The only son of this Mandavya died of snakebite. To save his life, they did 'Act of truth'. Krishna Dwipayana admitted that though he did not like the life of a saint, he took up this profession for glory. Mandavya's wife confessed that she stayed with her husband although she did not like him at all. Mandavya admitted that neither did he respect the saints nor did he donate them with pleasure. However, the boy recovered due to the 'Acts of the truth' by all concerned.

The Mahabharata's story goes like this. There was a pious saint named Mandavya who used to meditate under a tree in front of his hermitage. A few robbers, being chased by the security forces, hid around the cottage hiding the booty there. When the security guards came and questioned Mandavya, he could not reply as he was still under meditation. They mistook him for the leader of the robbers and took him to the king along with the booty and other robbers. The king got convinced that Mandavya was the ring leader of the robbers. He pronounced death sentence for Mandavya by impalement. Although Mandavya was impaled on a stake, he did not die and remained as it is for a long period. The king could realize the mistake and the stake protruding outside the body were cut. Mandavya went to Dharma (the god of religion) and asked him the reasons for such punishment. Dharma said that this punishment was accorded to him because he had impaled a straw on the hind side of an insect during his childhood. Mandavya opined that, this was an extreme punishment meted out for a small offence and that too, was committed at an age of insanity. He cursed that Dharma will have to be born in a lowest caste family and that sins or virtues of a person up to fourteen years of age shall not be counted for punishment or reward. In the Mahabharata, Dharma had to take birth in Sudra (lowest class as a sweeper) caste as 'Vidura'.

3.2.12 Ghata Jataka *(Ghaṭa Jātaka - 454)*

In the ancient days there was a kingdom in the northern India named Kamsa-bhog, where king Maha-kamsa used to reign. He had two sons named Kamsa and Upa-kamsa and a daughter named Devagarbha. On the birthday of Davagarbha, the Brahmins predicted that Devagarbha's son would kill Kamsa and destroy the country. When Maha-kamsa died, Kamsa became the king. He appointed Upa-kamsa as his viceroy. Being afraid of the prediction, Kamsa confined his sister Devagarbha in a separate tower in the palace. He did not even marry her off. A maid named Nandagopa was engaged to look after her. At that time a king named Mahasagara reigned in the north Mathura, who had two sons, Sagara and Upa-sagara. Upon Mahasagara's death, Sagara became the king and Upa-sagara the viceroy. Once Upa-sagara did some mischief with Sagara's wife and fled Mathura to take refuge in the Kamsa Kingdom. Upa-kamsa was the ex-classmate of Upa-sagara, who happily received him and introduced him to Kamsa. Kamsa showed great honours to him. Upa-sagara and Devagarbha fell in love with each other under mediation of Nandagopa. Upa-sagara met Devagarbha in her captivity and she conceived soon. On knowing this, Kamsa gave his sister married to Upa-sagara and allotted them a village named Govardamana. Devagarbha gave birth to a daughter named Anjana. As she was a girl, Kamsa spared her. Devagarbha conceived again and gave birth to a boy. On the same day, Nandagopa also gave birth to a daughter. Being afraid of Kamsa, the newborns were exchanged secretly. In this way, Devagarbha and Nandagopa gave births to ten sons and ten daughters respectively and exchanged them without the knowledge of others. Kamsa felt safe that Devagarbha did not give birth to any boy. Actually, Devagarbha's ten sons named Vasudeva, Baladeva, Chandradeva, Suryadeva, Agnideva, Varunadeva, Arjuna, Parjuna, Ghatapandita and Ankura grew up at their foster parents' (Nandagopa and Andhakavenhu) place and came to be known as the Ten-Slave Brothers. They were very powerful, ferocious and went on plundering. When confronted by the King, Andhakavenhu confessed that these were the sons of Devagarbha. To kill these ten brothers, Kamsa arranged for a wrestling contest and got two dreaded wrestlers named Chanura and Mustika. During the contest, the second brother Baladeva killed Chanura and Mustika in the ring. Mustika, while dying, took oath to become a Goblin in his next birth and kill Baladeva. Vasudeva's wheel chopped the heads of Kamsa and Upa-kamsa.

The ten brothers assumed the charge of the kingdom with Vasudeva at the helm. They invaded all the kingdoms in India and conquered all of them. They established their capital at Dwaravati and divided the kingdom into ten shares. Ankura gave his share to Anjana and took up to trading. In course of time, Vasudeva's beloved son died. This made Vasudeva half dead in grief. He kept on lamenting and neglecting everything. Ghatapandita, to sooth his elder brother, posed as half-mad, gazed towards the moon in the sky and kept on crying, "Give me the hare, which is in the moon." Vasudeva asked, how can you ask for the hare, which is seen in the moon? Ghatapandita shot back, "How can you get back your son, who is already dead?" Vasudeva came back to his senses. After passage of a long period, the sons of the ten brethren wanted to test the wisdom of the saint Krishha Dwipayana. They dressed up a boy like a pregnant Lady and went to the great saint. They asked him to tell as to when the 'Lady' would 'deliver'.

The saint, through foresight could know the trick. He could also visualise that he would be killed on that day by this group and the Vasudeva's clan would vanish thereafter. He replied that the person should deliver a wooden knot on the seventh day. Even if, they burn that wooden knot and throw the ashes in the river, it would cause the end of Vasudeva's dynasty. The boys, abusing the great saint as false recluse, pounced upon him and killed him. As foretold, the boy produced a wooden piece on the seventh day, which was burnt and the ash was thrown in the river. The ashes, after flowing for a while got struck on the bank and an Eraka plant born out of these. One day, the entire brethren went to the bank of the river to rejoice. They got drunk and started fighting with each other. They playfully plucked the leaves of the Eraka plant, which got converted into solid maces. They started beating each other and killed all excepting Vasudeva, Baladeva, Anjana and her chaplain. They went towards the forest in the chariot. While on the way, they met a goblin (Mustika, the wrestler, become this goblin), who ate away Baladeva. While tired Vasudeva was resting on the ground in a forest, a hunter (named Jara) mistook his feet for birds. His poisonous arrow pierced Vasudeva's foot and he died.

As per the Mahabharata, after 36 years of Yudhisthira's reign, one-day great saints Viswamitra, Kanva and Narada came to Dwaraka. A few Yadava kings hit upon a plan to test the wisdom of these great saints. They got Vasudeva's son Samba dressed up like a pregnant lady and took him to the saints. They asked the saints as to when 'She' would deliver a child. The saints could understand everything. They grew angry and pronounced that this son of Vasudeva shall deliver an iron mace, which will destroy all Yadavas except Vasudeva and Baladeva. Baladeva shall leave his earthly body and get into the ocean. The arrow of a Hunter named Jara shall kill Vasudeva. Next morning Samba produced an Iron Mace. This was crushed and the powder was thrown into the sea. All sorts of bad omen were sighted everywhere. Vasudeva's wheel left for heaven. His heavenly chariot also flew towards heaven. All the Yadavas came to the holy place 'Prabhasa'. But they started performing all unholy acts. They got completely drunk and started fighting with each other. They plucked the straws from seashore, which got converted into iron maces. They killed each other in free for all style. Vasudeva could recollect Gandhari's curse that the entire Yadu dynasty would be ruined. He could understand that the day has come. He did not try to protect any one. Rather, he picked up a mace himself and killed whoever was still alive. He sent his chaplain Daruka to bring Arjuna. Baladeva sat for meditation in the sea coast. A huge serpent came out of his mouth and went into the sea. His lifeless body laid there. Vasudeva went to a forest and lay down on a ground totally exausted. A hunter named Jara mistook his feet for bird and pierced the same with a poisonous arrow. He also expired and his soul left for heavenly abode.

The similarities between both the stories are very distinct.

3.2.13 Bhisa Jataka *(Bhisa Jātaka - 488)*

Once upon a time Bodhisattva had born in a rich householder family. He had six brothers, a sister, a maid, a servant and a friend. One day, all of them renounced the world and went to the Himalayas for meditation. They all stayed in individual huts built in an encircled form. Everymorning, one among the six brothers, servant and the friend used to go the forest to fetch fruits for all. After returning, he used to divide these in eleven parts and keep the same outside the huts and ring a bell. On hearing this bell, Individuals used to came out and collect his/her share. One day, the god-king Indra decided to test their virtue. He descended there and stole Bodhisattva's share of the lotus-stalks for three consecutive days. At this, all the members of the hermitage along with a neighbouring tree-god, an elephant and a monkey had a meeting. Everyone took oath stating that, he/she would harness worldly pleasure if he/she had stolen the food. The god king Indra came there and watched the proceedings without being noticed by anyone. Indra appeared before them and admitted to his role behind vanishing of lotus stalks. He praised the holiness of all persons.

As per the Mahabharata, seven great saints started meditating in the Himalayas. They were; Kassapa, Atri, Bharadwaj, Gautama, Viswamitra, Jamadagni and lady Arundhati. They had a maid named Ganda and her husband Pasusakh. Another fat recluse with his dog joined them. They went to a lake guarded by a female sprite, created to kill them. The sprite asked each to tell his/her name and meaning thereof before allowing them to get into the lake. When the turn came for the fat Recluse, he said that his name was 'Suna Sakhasama' (listen like a friend). The sprite got confused at this. When the confused sprite asked to repeat the name, the saint killed her with the trident. He then sat on the bank of the lake. The saints being extremely hungry fetched Lotus-stalks from the lake. They kept those on the bank and again got into the lake for bathing and offering prayers. When they returned, they found the Lotus-stalks were missing. Each one cursed the thief. Everyone took an oath that if he/she had stolen the lotus stalks, they would loose sainthood. The fat recluse said that the thief shall get his daughter married to the most learned Brahmin who takes bath only after reciting the Atharva Veda. The saints could understand that the oath was not a curse but a boon. The fat recluse accepted to stealing and revealed his true identity as the god-king Indra. He had come to test them as well as to save them. The saints were offered heavenly abode for their piousness.

Both the stories are similar.

3.2.14 Sibi Jataka *(Sivi Jātaka - 494)*

Once upon a time, Bodhisattva had born in the city of Aritrapura in the Sibi kingdom as son of the great king Sibi. After the death of his father, he ascended to the throne and came to be known as king Sibi. He followed the Ten Royal Virtues and ruled righteously. He used to donate everything generously. Once he thought that he would not even hesitate to donate his heart if anyone asked. On coming to know this, Indra come to test him in the disguise of an old blind Brahmin and requested him to donate one eye. King Sivi got excited. He donated both his eyes in spite of extreme pain. His doctor Jivaka transplanted the eyes in the Brahmin's body, which regained visibility. The king became blind. He renounced the throne and wanted to die. Indra appeared from his disguise and after realising that he had whole-heartedly donated his eyes, blessed him with divine eyes.

As per the Mahabharata, king Ushinara was holy minded and was famous for his charity. Gods Indra and Agni wanted to test his virtue. They disguised themselves in the form of a hawk and a pigeon respectively. The hawk chased the pigeon, which flew into king Ushinara's court and took refuge on the king's thigh. The chasing hawk also drove in and demanded the release of the pigeon, which was his legitimate meal. The king refused to part with the refugee and offered the hawk any alternative food he wished. The hawk demanded the flesh from the king's body of equivalent weight of the pigeon. A weighing scale was brought in the court of the king. The pigeon was put on one side of the scale and the king started cutting and putting the flesh from his own body on the other. Finding the pigeon's weight still heavier, the king himself sat on the other side of the balance. At this moment, both the gods appeared in their own forms and praised the king. The king thereafter, went to the heaven for his piousness.

The Jataka story is a slight variation of the story in the Mahabharata.

3.2.15 Alambusha Jataka *(Alambusa Jātaka - 523)*

An ascetic resided in a hermitage in a forest. A doe ate his semen mixed with grass and gave birth to a human-like boy. The hermit reared the boy and named him Rishishringa. The boy became an ascetic and his holiness excited the jealousy of god Indra, who sent a heavenly nymph by name Alambusha to seduce him. She did her job well and kept Rishishringa immersed in sensual pleasure for long three years. Thereafter, Rishishringa realized his mistake and restored to his previous holy life after leaving Alambusha.

3.2.16 Nalinika Jataka *(Nalinika Jātaka - 526)*

In this Jataka, the birth story of Rishishringa has been narrated as in Alambusa Jataka. Rishishringa's holiness bothered Indra, who hit upon a plan to deviate him from the virtuous path. There were draught in the kingdom of Kashi for three consecutive years. These brought in famine and severe sufferings on its inhabitants. On the advice of Indra, the king sent his daughter Nalinika to seduce the ascetic and immerse him in sexual pleasure. Nalinika played her role well and returned. As a result, rainfall resumed and the country was restored to normalcy. Rishishringa could realize the mistake and resumed his meditation.

As per the Mahabharata, a saint named Bibhandaka used to reside in a hermitage in a forest by the side of the 'Great Lake'. One day he saw a heavenly nymph named Urvashi to pass by. Her clothes were swept by the unruly wind. The saint could visualise her beautiful bare body. The saint was so much attracted to her beauty that he could not control himself. He discharged semen and washed himself in the adjoining Great Lake. A doe came to the lake for drinking water. It took the water mixed with semen and became pregnant. In due course of time, it gave birth to a human-like baby which had horns on its head. Bibhandaka kept the boy in his hermitage and grew him up as a saint. The boy was named as Rishyashringa, which literally means a saint (Rishi) having horn (Shringa). The kingdom of Anga was experiencing draught and severe famine because of unjust rules of its king Lompada. When he asked the priests about the remedy, they advised him to get saint Rishyashringa in his kingdom. The ascetic had never seen a lady earlier. He was easily seduced by a group of prostitutes, deployed by the king Lompada. They lured Rishishringa to the palace of the king. The king welcomed him and gave in his daughter Shanta married to him. Rain resumed and normalcy restored. Rishishringa continued to stay in the Anga kingdom alongwith his wife.

3.2.17 Kunala Jataka *(Kuṇāla Jātaka - 536)*

Brahmadatta, the King of Kashi invaded and won the state of Kosala. He killed the king of Kosala, took away his pregnant queen and made her his Queen-consort. The queen, in due course gave birth to a daughter named princess Krishna. When she grew up, she wanted to select her own husband. King Bramhadatta announced this in the Assembly. A *Sawamvar* function was arranged, so that the princess could choose her husband from an assemblage of kings/princes. Kings from various places attended the function. Five Pandava brothers were also present on the occasion. The princess was shameless and had excessive passion. She garlanded the five Pandava brothers and married all of them collectively. After marriage, she used to please all five brothers simultaneously. Additionally, she was also having illicit relationship with a humpback ugly servant. When her husbands came to know about her illicit affair, they renounced the world and went to the Himalayas as ascetics.

As per the Mahabharata, an archery competition was held as per the tradition to select husband for Draupadi or Krishna. The third Pandava, Arjun won the competition. Hence, Draupadi was supposed to marry Arjun. When the Pandava brothers reached home with Draupadi, they asked their mother Kunti to come out of the house and see what surprise they have brought for her. Kunti, without knowing, replied as usual that all five Pandava brothers must share the good thing together. This was the reason that Draupadi had to be married off to all five brothers. She was devoted to her husbands and never had any extra-marital relationship with anyone else. For her sacrifices, she is revered as a Sacred Lady in the Hindu mythology.

This sort of relationships of men and women were neither discouraged nor looked upon with as an evil in the society at the time of Mahabharata. However, Lord Buddha was opposed to such evil systems and he gave his message through the story accordingly. The story has lot of similarities with the story of the Mahabharata but has been recast in line with the Buddhist philosophy.

3.2.18 Maha-sutasoma Jataka *(Mahasutasoma Jātaka - 537)*

Bodhisattva had born to the Queen-consort of the king Kauravya in the city of Indraprastha. It was the capital of kingdom of Kuru. The new-born was named as 'Sutasoma'. When he grew up, he studied at Takshasila along with the prince of Kashi, named Brahmadatta-kumara. Later on, both became kings of their respective kingdoms. Bramhadatta was a Yaksha in his previous birth and as such he was very much fond of meat. One day, his cook could not get meat for the king and instead cooked and served the flesh of a human body collected from the cemetery. The king could recognise the taste and thenceforth become a regular man-eater. He ultimately left the kingdom and kept wondering in the forest in search of human flesh. He caught one hundred kings and kept them captive for sacrifice. Ultimately, he abducted Sutasoma also. Sutasoma said that he had promised to a Brahmin to listen to his verses. He requested Brahmadatta to release him for some time and assured him to return to his captivity. He went back, heard the Brahmin, rewarded him and came back to Brahmadatta's captivity. The cannibal was surprised at this. Sutasoma gave him good advice and transformed the man-eater. He released the captivated Kings and returned to normal life.

As in the Mahabharata, Kalmashpada was a decendent from the Ikshashu dynasty and a great king. Great saints Vasistha and Viswamitra were in competition with each other to rope in the king as their disciple. One day, the tired king was returning to the palace through a narrow walkway in a forest. Srakti, the eldest son of saint Vasistha, was also coming from the opposite side. The king ordered him to leave the way for him. Srakti politely reminded the king that as per the rule, the Kshatriyas should respect the

Brahmins. Hence, he should make way for Srakti. At this, the king got annoyed and he whipped Srakti. Srakti cursed king Kalmaspada that he would become a man-eater demon. At that moment, saint Viswamitra appeared and induced a demon in the king's body. The king's mind got transformed accordingly. Further, on his way home, he met a Brahmin. The Brahmin wanted to have food with meat from king Kalmaspada. Upon reaching the palace, the king forgot about the Brahmin waiting for food. In the midnight only he could recollect about it and instructed the cook accordingly. The cook could not arrange meat at that hour. In absence of meat, the king asked his cook to prepare the food with human flesh. When this food was served to the Brahmin, he again cursed the king to become a man-eater. King again happened to meet Srakti. As instigated by his Guru Viswamitra, king Kalmaspada first ate Srakti and then other ninety-nine sons of ascetic Vasistha. Vasistha tried to commit suicide in all possible ways but could not die. Kalmaspada Later chased Vasistha's daughter-in-law Adrisanti, who was carrying at that time. Seeing the problem, Vasistha sprinkled the holy water on the man-eater king and relived him from the curse to restore normalcy.

Here, the story of the Mahabharata has been modified substantially.

3.2.19 Kurudharma Jataka *(Kurudhamma Jātaka - 276)*

In this Jataka, the names used in the Mahabharata such as; Kuru kingdom, Indraprastha city, Korava clan, Dhananjaya king etc. have been used.

However, there are very little or no similarities with the stories of the Mahabharata.

3.2.20 Dhumkari Jataka *(Dhumkāri Jātaka - 413)*

This Jataka also used various names from the Mahabharata but there are no similarities between the stories of both the books.

3.2.21 Dasabrahmana Jataka *(Dasabrahmaṇa Jātaka - 495)* Sambhava Jataka *(Sambhava Jātaka - 515)*

These Jatakas contain names from the Mahabharata but there are no similarities with the stories of Mahabharata.

3.2.22 Sankha-pala Jataka *(Samkhapāla Jātaka - 524)*

This Jataka contains the name of the king Durjodhana of Mahabharata but there are no other similarities.

3.2.23 Chulla-hansa Jataka *(Cullahamsa Jātaka - 533)* Maha-hansa Jataka *(Mahāhamsa Jātaka - 534)*

The troop of geese is named after 'Yudhisthira' and the Commander-in-Chief after 'Sumukha'. These are the famous names in the Mahabharata. There are no other similarities.

3.2.24 Vidurapandita Jataka *(Vidurapaṇḍiṭa Jātaka - 545)*

This Jataka contains names similar to the Mahabharata, such as; Kuru kingdom, King Dhananjaya, Priest Vidura etc. There is also similarity in playing the game of dice keeping the entire Kingdom at stake.

The foregoing comparisons clearly bring out that the links between the Mahabharata and the Jataka.

ASCETIC (KING) BHARATA WITH NEW BORN FAWN

3.3 Jataka and the Bhagabata

The Bhagabata is the life story of the god 'Vishnu', who descended on the earth on various occasions in various forms or 'Avataras' to rid this world from injustice. As per the tradition, the compilation of the Bhagabata also dates back to the pre-Buddha era. Since his birth as Lord Krishna or Kanha, he played a vital role in the Mahabharata. Many incidences narrated in the Bhagabata also found place in the great epic. Common incidents narrated in both the compilations are sequential and perfectly match each other. They do not suffer from inconsistencies or differences whatsoever.

We shall now bring fourth only those Jataka stories, which have resemblances with the Bhagabata and have not appeared in the previous chapter titled "Jataka and the Mahabharata."

3.3.1 Mriga-potaka Jataka *(Migapotaka Jātaka - 372)*

Once upon a time, king Brahmadatta reigned in Benares. Bodhisattva was god Indra. A person got converted as a recluse and dwelt in a hermitage in the Himalayas. One day, he found an orphaned fawn. He brought it to his cottage and reared it up with great affection, as if it were his own son. In due course, it grew up to a beautiful deer. One day it died from indigestion caused by over-eating. The ascetic was deeply shocked and kept on mourning and lamenting. Seeing this, the god king Indra came to him and said that the ascetic had earlier freed himself from all worldly ties and became a recluse but now got entangled with worldly woes and was mourning for an animal. Hearing this, the ascetic regained his senses and resorted to meditation once again.

As per the Bhagabata, king Bharata, after reigning for a long period renounced the world and came to a hermitage and took up the life of an ascetic. One day, while he was offering prayer standing half-immersed in a river, a pregnant doe, hearing the roaring of a lion, jump crossed the river and died. The developed foetus came out of her body and fell in the river water in front of Bharata. He picked it up and a fawn had born out of it. Bharata started raring up the fawn with great care and affection. He gradually became so much involved in the affection of the deer that he totally forgot about his meditation. One day the deer left him and went to the jungle. Bharata felt extremely distressed about this and died thinking about its welfare. Because of this, in his next birth he had to be born as a deer.

The Jataka story is similar to the story of the Bhagabata with minor deviations.

3.3.2 Ghata Jataka *(Ghaṭa Jātaka - 454)*

In the ancient days there was a kingdom in the northern India named Kamsa-bhog, where king Maha-kamsa used to reign. He had two sons named Kamsa and Upa-kamsa and a daughter named Devagarbha. On the birthday of Davagarbha, the Brahmins predicted that her son would kill Kamsa and destroy the country. When Maha-kamsa died, Kamsa became the King and he made Upa-kamsa his Viceroy. Kamsa kept Devagarbha confined in a separate tower in the palace and she was not married off. A maid named Nandagopa was engaged to look after her. At that time, a king named Mahasagara reigned in the north Mathura, who had two sons, Sagara and Upa-sagara. Upon Mahasagara's death, Sagara became the King and Upa-sagara the Viceroy. Once Upa-sagara did some mischief with Sagara's wife and left Mathura to take refuge in Kamsa

Kingdom. Upa-kamsa was the classmate of Upa-sagara who happily received him and introduced to Kamsa. Kamsa showed great honours to him and he thereafter started residing in Kamsa-bhog. Upa-sagara and Devagarbha fell in love with each other under mediation of Nandagopa. Upa-sagara kept on meeting Debagarbha in her captivity and she conceived soon. On knowing this, Kamsa gave his sister married to Upa-sagara and allotted them a village by name Gobardhamana. Debagarva gave birth to a daughter and named her Anjana. Since, it was a girl, Kamsa spared her. Devagarbha conceived again and gave birth to a boy. On the same day Nandagopa also gave birth to a daughter. Being afraid of Kamsa, the children were exchanged secretly. In this way, Devagarbha and Nandagopa gave births to ten sons and ten daughters and exchanged them without the knowledge of others. Kamsa felt safe that Devagarbha did not give birth to any boy. Actually, Devagarbha's ten sons named Vasudeva, Baladeva, Chandradeva, Suriyadeva, Agnideva, Varunadava, Arjuna, Parjuna, Ghatapandita and Ankura grew up at their foster parents' (Nandagopa and Andhakavenhu) place and came to be known as the Ten Slave-brothers. They were very powerful, ferocious and went on plundering. When confronted by the King, Andhakavenhu confessed that these were actually the sons of Devagarbha. To kill these ten brothers, Kamsa arranged for a wrestling contest and got two dreaded wrestlers Chanura and Mustika. The second brother Baladeva killed both Chanura and Mustika in the ring. Mustika, while dying, took an oath to become a Goblin in his next birth and kill Baladeva. Vasudeva's wheel chopped the heads of Kamsa and Upa-kamsa.

The ten brothers assumed the charge of the kingdom with Vasudeva at the helm. They invaded all the kingdoms in India and conquered all of them. They established their capital at Dwaravati and divided the kingdom into ten shares. Ankura gave his shave to sister Anjana and took up to trading. In course of time, Vasudeva's beloved son died. This made him half dead in grief. He kept on lamenting and neglecting everything. Ghatapandita, to sooth his elder brother, posed as half-mad, gazed towards the moon in the sky and kept on crying, "Give me the hare." Vasudeva asked, how could you ask for the hare, which in the moon? Ghatapandita shot back, "How can you get back your son, who is already dead?" Vasudeva came back to his senses. After passage of a long period, the sons of the ten brethren wanted to test the wisdom of the great saint Krishna Dwipayana. They dressed up a boy like a pregnant lady and went to the great saint. They asked him to tell as to when the "Lady" would deliver. The saint through his foresight could know everything and that he would die on that day and the Vasudeva's clan would vanish thereafter. He replied that the person should deliver a wooden knot on the seventh day. He proclaimed, even if, they burnt that wooden knot and threw the ashes in the river, would cause the end of Vasudeva's dynasty. The boys, abusing the great saint as false recluse, pounced upon him and killed him. As foretold, the boy produced a wooden piece on the seventh day, which was burnt and the ash was thrown in the river. The ashes, after flowing for a while got struck on the bank and *Eraka* plants born out of these. One day, the entire brethren went to the bank of the river to rejoice. They got drunk and started fighting with each other playfully. They plucked the leaves of Eraka plant, which became solid maces. They started hitting each other and killed all excepting Vasudeva, Baladeva, Anjana and her chaplain. They went away in the chariot. On the way, they met a goblin (Mustika, the wrestler become this goblin), who ate away Baladeva. While Vasudeva was resting on the ground in a forest, a hunter (named Jara) mistook his feet for a bird. He released a poisonous arrow, which pierced Vasudeva's foot and he died.

As in the Bhagabata, Kamsa was the son of king Ugrasena. He was a very cruel and notorious ruler. Kamsa's sister Devaki got married to king Vasudeva. After the marriage, Vasudeva set for his home together with his wife in a chariot. Devaki's brother king Kamsa was driving it. Suddenly, there was an Oracle from the heaven that Devaki's eighth son would kill Kamsa. Infuriated Kamsa immediately attempted to kill Devaki but was dissuaded by Vasudeva. He promised to handover all their children to Kamsa as soon as they were born. Kamsa kept Devaki and Vasudeva imprisoned with their hands and feet chained in the underground prison beneath his palace. Kamsa also imprisoned his father Ugrasena. Kamsa killed the first seven sons of Devaki as soon as they were born. Ultimately, Lord Vishnu descended and took birth as the eighth son of Devaki.

Simultaneously, Goddess Yogamaya took birth in Gokula as the daughter to king Nanda's wife Yasoda. On that night, there was extreme inclement weather with torrential rain and thunderstorm and the entire world fell asleep. Vasudeva got an oracle to take his son to Gokula and exchange him with Nanda's newborn daughter. All the chains got detached from his body and the prison gate became wide open. Vasudeva took his son in arms and went to Gokula crossing the river *Yamuna.* A huge serpent spread its hood like an umbrella above the head of Vasudeva to protect the baby and escorted him. Vasudeva laid his son by the side of Yashoda and picked up her daughter and returned to the prison cell. Again the chains got attached to his body and the prison gates got closed and locked automatically. The inclement weather also disappeared and the atmosphere got normalized. Kamsa got the news of Devaki's delivery. He came running, picked up the baby girl and threw her on a stone to kill her. The baby, in stead of falling on the stone and getting killed, went up in air, took the shape of the goddess Yogamaya. She told Kamsa that, his killer had already born elsewhere and would kill him at the appropriate time.

Devaki's son was named as Krishna or Kanha and grew up in Gokula as Yashoda's son. He later came to Mathura with his elder brother Balarama and other friends. Kamsa had arranged for a wrestling competition, where dreaded wrestlers named Chanura, Mustika, Kuta, Sala, Tosala etc. were brought to kill Krishna and his team. But Krishna and Balarama killed all the wrestlers. They also killed Kamsa and his eight brothers. Later, they met Vasudeva and Devaki in the underground prison and freed them.

Thus the Jataka story resembles the story of the Bhagabata. In the Jataka, Kamsa is shown as a great pious ruler and Devagarbha's (Devaki in the Bhagabata) sons as cruel, notorious and unruly characters. As per Bhagabata, Kamsa was the most notorious, cruel and unjust ruler of Mathura. To get rid of him and to establish the righteous rule, god Vishnu himself had to descend upon the earth in the form of Sri Krishna.

3.3.3 Nimi Jataka *(Nimi Jātaka - 541)*

Once upon a time, a king named Makhadeva reigned in the city of Mithila in the kingdom of Videha. He ruled righteously for quite a long period. When his hair started greying, he renounced the throne and took to the life of an ascetic. All his successors also followed the same tradition. He watched this for many ages from the heaven and decided to take birth again in the world. This time he took his birth as prince Nimi. When he ascended to the throne, he had a query in his mind, "Which is more virtuous, either 'Charity' or the 'life of an ascetic'?" God-king Indra came to know about his query. He came to Nimi and explained that "Brahmacharya" or leading ascetic's life was even more virtuous than charity. When Indra apprised the inhabitant of the heaven about King Nimi, they showed interest to see him. Indra sent his chariot with charioteer Matali to Nimi to bring him to the heaven. Accordingly, Matali reached to him with the chariot. As invited by Indra, Nimi boarded the chariot. While travelling to the heaven in the chariot, he went via hell. Matali kept on explaining him the various punishments prescribed for various types of offences to the sinners. He also showed king Nimi the various palaces and the facilities in the heaven being enjoyed by the persons who performed pious deeds. After staying for a while and meeting the gods in the heaven, Nimi returned to his kingdom and narrated his experience to the others.

In the Bhagabata, description of the hell and the various punishments prescribed for different types of offences are depicted, which matches with the narrations in the Jataka.

As per the Bhagabata, king Nimi once performed a *Yagna* or worship. Nine prominent saints came on the occasion. The king was extremely pleased and welcomed them with great honour. He then asked them various questions on Virtue, to which they happily replied. This resembles Indra's answering Nimi's queries in the Jataka.

THE FOUR FRIENDS

3.4 Jataka and the Panchatrantra

Panchatantra is a collection of fables written in the ancient days in Sanskrit. Panchatantra owes its origin to the 'Nitisastra'. 'Pancha' means five and 'tantra' means code of conduct. Panchatantra depicts Nitisastra in the form of fables involving mainly animal characters. It is said to have been composed in the post-Buddha era. Interestingly, many of its stories are similar to those in the Jataka. It seems that these fables might have been borrowed from the Jataka. We shall enjoy the similar stories written in both the works.

3.4.1 Baka Jataka *(Baka Jātaka - 38)*

A crane lived near a lotus pond full of fishes. He hit upon a plan to eat as much fish as he wished. He stood in the pond thoughtfully. When asked by the group of fishes, he told that he was worried about their welfare since the water of the pond was receding. He offered to carry them to a big lake, where they could live much better life. When they expressed their apprehension, the crane assured that he would not eat them. He took a large blind fish to the so called 'Lake' and brought him back. The fish, being blind, could not see anything. To hide his shortcomings, he portrayed an imaginery "beauty of that lake to the others". All the fishes got convinced to the crane's story and agreed to be carried there. The crane carried one fish at time in his beaks and instead of taking them to lake, took them on the branch of a tree and ate them. In this process he ate all the fishes of the pond. Only a crab remained there. The crane also offered to transport him to the bigger lake like others. The crab doubted the honesty of the crane and wanted to be transported hanging on the cranes neck instead of the beaks. The unsespecting crane agreed to the proposal. As usual, the crane started flying with him away from the lake and told him on the way that he would devour the crab as he had done to the other fishes, the crab already had this apprehension and that's why bargained to be carried hanging on the neck. He tightened his grip on the Crane's neck with his sharp claws like pincers and chopped the crane's head off his body.

As in the Panchtantra, there lived a stork by the side of a tank full of fishes. When the stork grew old, he was almost unable to catch fishes for his meal. He hit upon a plan to catch the fishes without efforts. One day, he stood in the tank and looked sad. He even did not make any effort to catch the fishes, who passed by him. When asked, he explained that the tank would soon be filled in to grow corps.

Listening this, the fishes, frogs and crabs got worried and asked for the way out. The stork volunteered to carry them to a large and deeper tank. Believing this, they got ready to be transported. The stork carried a few fishes at a time in his beaks and instead of releasing them in the tank, took them to a rock and devoured them. He then returned and made the next trip as before. There lived a big crab in the tank. He also requested the stork to carry him. The stork thought it could be the right time to try a crab now for a change. The crab being of odd shape, preferred to be transported clinging to the neck of the crab. The stork flew merrily with the crab clinging to his neck. The crab tried to locate the larger tank, which was going to be his new abode. But he could not find any water down below. The Stork started descending on a rock. The crab enquired about the beautiful lake. At this, the stork laughed loudly and told him that he was carrying him to the rock for a meal. The crab could find the rock below was strewn with fish bones. He dug his sharp claws on the neck of the stork, cut his head. He then dragged it back to the tank and narrated the stork's cheating to his remaining friends there.

Both the versions are almost identical.

3.4.2 Mitachinti Jataka *(Mitacinti Jātaka - 114)*

Once upon a time, there lived three fishes in a river near Benares. They were named Bahuchinti (over-thoughtful), Alpachinti (less-thoughtful) and Mitachinti (proper-thoughtful). Earlier, they had been living in the jungle areas, where no fishermen ever ventured. Now, they swam near human-infested town, where, chances of getting caught in the net were distinct. Mitachinti cautioned his friends about the impending danger and requested them to go elsewhere. But the two others were enjoying stay over there, since they were getting better food and were reluctant to move out. One day, foolish Bahuchinti and Alpachinti got trapped in the fishermen's net. Seeing this, Mitachinti played a trick and freed his friends.

As per the Mahabharata, three fishes lived in a pond. Their names were, Anagata Bidhata (foresighted), Pratyutpannamati (intelligent) and Dirgha-Sutra (slow-going). One day the fishermen started dewatering the pond. Anagata Bidhata cautioned the two friends and said, "Let us go out now taking the canal route, or else, we will be trapped". Pratyutpannamati said, "Don't worry, I shall find a way out at the nick of the moment" Dirgha-Sutra opined "We need not hurry about anything now". Anagata Bidhata swam to safety to another reservoir. When the water in the pond receded, the fishermen caught all the fishes and passed a rope through their mouths like a garland. Pratyutpannamati was yet to be joined in that garland. He voluntarily bit the rope strongly pretending that he too had been tied in the rope. When the fishermen took the rope with the fishes to a big reservoir for washing, he escaped to safety. Dirgha-Sutra could not go anywhere and was killed.

As per the Panchatantra, three fishes lived in a pond. They were named Anagata-bidhata (foresighted), Pratyutpanna-mati (intelligent) and Yadhvavisya (believer in the destiny). The Anagata-bidhata heard fishermen talking that they would be fishing in this lake. He cautioned his friends and suggested them to leave for another lake through a canal. Pratyutpanna-mati replied that he was intelligent enough and would find out a way when the need arose. Yadhavisya preferred not a worry and to leave the future to the fate. Anagata-bidhata went to the other lake through the canal. The other two were caught in the fishermen's net. Pratyutpanna-mati pretended to be dead and was thrown by the fishermen over a heap of dead Fishes. From there she jumped back in the lake and was saved. Yadhavisya had to die in the hands of the fishermen.

Stories of the Jataka, the Mahabharata and the Panchatantra are similar. However, the stories of the Mahabharata and the Panchatantra have much more similarities including the names and hence the story of the Panchatantra might have emanated from the Mahabharata.

3.4.3 Sanjiva Jataka *(Sañjīva Jātaka - 150)*

Once upon a time Bodhisattva was a world-renowned teacher in Benares. One of his pupils named Sanjiva learnt from him the lesson of bringing back the dead to life. One day, Sanjiva and a few other pupils had gone to the forest to collect wood. Finding a dead tiger lying there, Sanjiva said that he would bring it to life. Hearing this, other pupils got up a tree. As soon as Sanjiva performed the charm, the tiger came back to life. On getting life, he found Sanjiva in front of him. He immediately pounced on Sanjiva and killed him and also lay dead again. Other pupils, getting down from the tree, went to the teacher and narrated him the incident.

As per the Panchatantra, there lived four friends. Three of them had good knowledge but lacked common sense. The fourth one did not have much knowledge but had the required common senses. One day, while roaming in a forest, they found the remains of a lion. The learned friends tried to bring it back to life, while the fourth one climbed up a nearby tall tree. One friend assembled the bones, the second one added flesh, skin and blood and the third one inducted life in it. The Lion came to life and finding the three friends in front of him, pounced on them and killed them.

Both the stories are similar. The story of Panchatantra might have been derived from the Jataka story.

3.4.4 Kuranga-mriga Jataka *(Kuraṅgamiga Jātaka - 206)*

Once upon a time Bodhisattva came to life as an antelope. He used to reside in a thicket of a forest by the side of a lake. There also lived a woodpecker in a nearby tree and a tortoise in the lake. The three were good friends. One day, a hunter laid a trap and the antelope got trapped in it. The bird and the tortoise immediately embarked upon the rescue mission. While the tortoise kept on biting the leather trap to cut it, the bird flew to the hunter's house to keep him at bay as long as possible. When the hunter came out of his house through front door in the dawn, the bird flew towards him, flapping his wings on his face with a shriek. The hunter, considering it a bad omen, went back to bed for a while and started again after a while through the rear door. The bird again repeated the act. The hunter, again, considering it a bad omen slept till sunrise. Seeing the hunter moving thereafter, the bird went back and informed his friends. By then, the tortoise had almost cut the trap. The antelope gave a jerk with full might, freed himself and ran to a distance. The tortoise was bleeding profusely following his incessant attempt to chew the leather trap and was too weak to move out quickly. The hunter found the trap lying empty. He also discovered that the tortoise was lying there. He murmered to himself, "Something is better than nothing". He caught the tortoise and put him in his bag. Watching this, the antelope tempted the hunter standing at a comfortable distance. The hunter tied the opening of the bag and threw the bag there. He ran after the antelope to catch him. Having lured away the hunter to a substantial long distance, the antelope sped back to the bag, tore it with the help of his horns and freed the turtle. The tortoise, getting time walked to the lake and dove back in the depth of it. Thus they saved themselves.

As per the Panchatantra, there lived four friends; a mouse, a crow, a tortoise and a deer in a forest near a lake. One morning, not finding the deer in them, the crow flew and found him trapped in a hunter's net. The crow came back quickly. He took the mouse on his back and flew back to the spot. The mouse promptly cut the net and set the deer free. The tortoise also crawled all the way to reach there. When the four friends were discussing, the hunter arrived there. The mouse hid himself in a hole, the crow went up a tree, and the deer ran to a safe distance. The tortoise, however, could not make it to the bush. The hunter found the net empty. Seeing the tortoise, he caught and put him in his bag and proceeded to his home. Watching this, the deer appeared on the path of the hunter maintaining a safe distance. The hunter left the bag there and chased the deer. The mouse quickly got into the action and cut open the bag and freed the turtle. The turtle walked quickly and hid himself in the thicket of the bush. The hunter could not catch the deer. When he returned, the turtle also had disappeared. He left for the home with the empty bag totally exhausted and disappointed.

Both the stories are similar. The Panchatantra story is a refined version of the Jataka.

3.4.5 Kachhapa Jataka *(Kacchapa Jātaka - 215)*

Once upon a time a tortoise dwelt in a lake in the Himalayan region. He grew friendship with two wild geese. One day, the geese decided to take their friend tortoise to their abode in the beautiful Chitrakuta plateau. Both the geese held a stick in their beaks. The turtle hung biting the stick from the middle. Before flying, they asked the tortoise not to open his mouth under any circumstances. While they were overflying the locality, boys on the ground below started telling each other about the unprecedented event. Hearing this, the tortoise got angry and he tried to scold the boys. As soon as he opened his mouth, he fell on the ground and split into two halves.

The story in the Panchatantra goes like this. A tortoise lived in a pond. He had two geese friends. Once, there was a severe drought and every one shifted to a safer place. The geese offered to take their friend tortoise to a better place hanging him from a stick held in their beaks. They cautioned him not to open his mouth under any circumstances while flying. They held a stick with their beaks and asked the tortoise to hold on to it by biting firmly. Soon they were airborne and kept flying. When they were passing over a locality, the boys on the ground raised a hue and cry seeing the strange scene. The tortoise wanted to shut them up. No sooner than he opened his mouth, he fell on the ground and got killed.

Both the stories are same.

3.4.6 Kuta-banijya Jataka *(Kūṭa-vāṇija Jātaka - 218)*

Long time ago, two traders, one from a village and the other from a town were friends. Once, the trader from the village came to his friend in the town and kept five hundred ploughshares with him. He said he would be back after a few days. When he went away, the townsman sold these and kept the money with him. He then sprinkled some mouse-dung in the storage place. When the villager returned and asked for the ploughshares, he showed him the place filled with the mouse-dung and said that the mice had eaten the ploughshares. The villager understood this simple story but did not say anything. He took the little son of the townsman with him to the bathing ghat. But instead of going to the river, he went to another friend's house and kept his friend's son there. He then returned to the townsman and reported that a hawk had carried away his son from the riverbank. The townsman could not believe this cock and bull story and took his friend to the court for justice. The Judge asked as to how a hawk could carry away a boy? The villager replied that if the mice could eat the ploughshares, why not a hawk could carry away his friend's son. On enquiry by the Judge, he narrated the story to the Judge. The Judge ordered the townsman to return the ploughshares and villager the boy. They did accordingly and the case got settled amicably.

As per the story of Panchatantra, a rich Trader named Nanduka suddenly turned poor and kept a heavy Iron beam with his friend Laxmana. When he returned, Laxmana informed him that the mice had eaten up the Iron beam.

Nanduka asked him friend not to bother about it and told him to send his son along with him to fetch a gift from his house, which he had brought for his friend. He took the boy to his home and confined him in a cellar. When his friend asked for his son, he said that on the way a hawk has carried off his son. His friend disbelieved him and dragged him to the Court of law. Nanduka told the Judge that if the mice could eat Iron, the hawk could also carry a person. He narrated the story to the Judge, who ordered both the persons to return each other's belongings.

There is hardly any difference between both the stories.

3.4.7 Vanarindra Jataka *(Vānarinda Jātaka - 57)*

Long time ago, Bodhisattva had born as a monkey and lived in the bank of a river. He was very strong and stout. There was an island in middle of the river, which was full of trees with varieties of ripe fruits. In between the island and the bank was a rock. Every morning the monkey used to jump from the bank to the rock and thence to the island. He used to enjoy tasty ripe fruits to his heart's content throughout the day. Every evening he used to return in the same route. There lived a crocodile couple in the river. Seeing the healthy monkey, the female crocodile longed to eat his heart and requested his mate for the same. Accordingly, the male crocodile rose on the rock in the evening and lay in wait for the monkey to return. The monkey, before jumping from the island noticed that the height of the rock had increased. He had some apprehensions. He asked the rock loudly, "Hi rock! Hi rock! Why are you not talking to me today?" The stupid crocodile thought that the rock must have been talking to him daily. So he replied, "Hi monkey! How are you?" The monkey enquired who was he and why was he sitting there.

The crocodile revealed his identity and said that he was sitting there to catch the monkey and to take his delicious heart for his wife as her dinner. The monkey asked him to open his mouth so that he could jump directly into his jaws. When a crocodile opens his jaws, the eyelids get shut. The crocodile obeyed the monkey, who took this opportunity. He did a hop-step jump, first stepping on the head of the Crocodile and thence making it to the shore. Since the eyes of the crocodile were shut, he could neither see nor catch the monkey.

3.4.8 Sisumara Jataka *(Sumsumāra Jātaka - 208)* Vanara Jataka *(Vānara Jātaka - 342)*

In these Jatakas, Bodhisattva had born as a monkey and used to live in a forest adjacent to the river Ganges on the foothills of the Himalayas. He grew strong and sturdy and lived on the fruits of the trees that grew on the bank of the river. A crocodile couple lived in the river. The female crocodile expressed to his mate that she longed to eat the heart of the monkey. The crocodile planned to catch the monkey. He lured the monkey saying that there were varieties of fruits available on the other side of the river. The monkey said that he could not swim. The crocodile offered to ferry him on his back. The monkey, believing the crocodile sailed on his back.

After a while, the crocodile started sinking. When the monkey enquired, the crocodile replied that he was taking him to his under-water home as his mate wanted to eat his heart. The monkey promptly replied, we keep our hearts on the fig trees, otherwise, when we keep on jumping from one tree to the other, these would be knocked down to the pieces. He then, pointing to a fig tree with ripe fruits on the bank, told that his heart was kept there. The monkey asked the croc to take him there, so that he could pluck his heart from the tree and gave the same to him. The crocodile believed the monkey and took him to the shore. The monkey leapt off his back on to a tree and exclaimed that the crocodile was indeed a great fool.

As per the story of Panchatantra, a monkey lived on a rose-apple tree on the bank of a river. A crocodile lived in the river, which grew friendship with the monkey. The monkey used to give him lot of rose apples every day. The crocodile carried some of the fruits for his mate. The female crocodile ate all the fruits, which were very sweet and tasty. One day she feigned illness and told her mate that the doctor had advised her that she would survive only if she could eat a monkey's heart. The male crocodile did not like this proposal but ultimately had to bow down before his mate's wishes. He went to the monkey as usual and said that his mate intends to see him. The crocodile also said that they stay on the other side of the river and he could carry the monkey there on his back. The unsuspecting monkey agreed to the proposal and sat on the crocodile's back. When they reached the mid river, the crocodile started sinking. When the frightened monkey enquired, the crocodile said that he was carrying him to his abode under water to offer his friend's heart to his wife. The monkey said, "You should have told me this before we set out. Before coming, I kept my heart on the Rose apple tree. Let us go back quickly and get the heart before the condition of your wife worsens". The crocodile about-turned immediately and swam swiftly to the shore. On reaching, the monkey jumped off the crocodile-back and perched himself safely on a branch of the tree. He told the crocodile, "Go and tell your wicked wife that, you are the biggest fool on this earth".

In another story of the Panchatantra, a hungry lion roamed in the forest but could not get any prey. He reached the entrance of a cave. He went inside and lay in wait for its inhabitants. A jackal used to live in that cave, who went out earlier in search of food. When he came back, he noticed the footprints of some big animal leading to his den. To know, who it was, he hit upon a plan. He called out loudly, "Hello cave! Hello dear cave! Why are you not welcoming me like other days? Is there any problems?" The lion heard the jackal and thought that the cave must be welcoming him every day but was silent today in the fear of the lion. He also thought that the jackal might go away if he were not welcomed. Hence the lion roared, "Hello, hello! Welcome home my dear friend." "He must be hungry indeed", amused was the wise jackal and fled the place as fast as he could.

The crocodile's story of the Panchatantra is similar to Sisumara Jataka (208) and Vanara Jataka (342). This story also matches partially with the Vanarindra Jataka (57). The other Panchatantra story of the 'Cave that talked' is similar to the second part of the Vanarindra Jataka (57).

TEACHER VISHNUSHARMA AND HIS STUDENTS

3.5 Jataka and the Hitopadesha

'Hitopadesha' means beneficial advices. It is said that, a king named Sudarshana reigned in the city of Pataliputra, situated on the bank of the river Bhagirathi. He had three stupid sons, who neither studied not were interested in it. They were extremely ill mannered and void of good senses. No teacher could ever teach them. The teachers had to run away due to the misbehaviour of the princes. There lived a great scholar named Visnusharma in that kingdom, who took the responsibility of teaching the princes the ethical values and principles of life. He started teaching them the moral and ethical values in the form of story telling. The boys found these stories very interesting and listened to the teacher very minutely. Visnushrama sourced these fables basically from the Panchatantra and others. The lessons imparted by Visnushama are compiled as the 'Hitopadesha', which is also known as an offspring of the Panchatantra. We shall take a tour through those similar stories of the Hitopadesa and the Jataka, which we did not come accross in the previous chapter.

3.5.1 Triparjasta-mriga Jataka *(Tipallattha-miga Jātaka - 16)*

Once upon a time, Bodhisattva had born in a forest as the head of a herd of deer. He taught a young stag the ruses of deer for self-protection. One day, the stag was caught in a snare and applied the ruses taught to him. He did not struggle to free himself, laid down on his side with legs fully stretched, taut and rigid. He pawed up the grass and earth around the hoofs, relieved nature, let his head fall, lolled out his tongue, slavered his body all over, swelled himself by inhaling wind, rolled up eyes, breathed lightly through lower nostrils and withheld breathing with upper nostrils. He stiffened his body to look like a corpse. Even the bluebottles swarmed around him and a few crows walked over his body. The hunter came and smacked the stag on the belly. He took him for dead, released the snare and started gathering the wood for feast. Seeing him unmindful, the stag rose to his feet and vanished swiftly in the thickets of the forest.

As in the Hitopadesha, a crow and a deer had friendship. A jackal also befriended them to slaughter and eat the meat of the deer. He lured the deer to graze in a cornfield. The deer went there daily. The landlord, noticing this, set a snare. The deer was caught in the snare the next day. He requested the jackal to cut it with his teeth and release him. But the jackal was happy to see the deer got trapped. He thought that he would get enough from the remains even after the landlord had taken out flesh from the deer's body. He told the deer that the day being a Sunday; he could not touch the leather trap with his mouth, since he observed fast on that day. Saying so, the jackal went away from the deer's view but lay in wait in a nearby bush. The crow, searching for the deer, reached the spot and found him trapped. The crow noticed that the landlord was approaching the spot with a stick in his hand. He advised the deer to lay stretched with legs stiffened and belly filled with air, posing as dead. The deer did so. The crow also said that he would make a signalling sound at an opportune moment. On hearing that, the deer should get up and run away. The landlord, on reaching to the spot, thought that the deer was dead. He removed the snare and got busy collecting dried haystocks for the feast. The crow signalled his friend at the most opportune moment. The deer sprang to his feet and ran away to freedom at a great speed. The landlord seeing the deer running away threw his stick. The stick missed the deer and hit the jackal, hidden in the bush. The jackal died.

Both the stories are similar.

3.5.2 Sammodamana Jataka *(Sammodamāna Jātaka - 33)*

In the ancient days, once Bodhisattva had born as a leader of thousands of quails. A fowler came with his net to catch the quails. He first imitated the note of a quail, so that they got down and assembled together at one place. He then cast his net over them. As already taught by their leader, the quails put their heads up through the mesh of the net and flew together in unison with the net. They got down on a thorn-brake and entangling the net on it, escaped through the bottom. The unlucky fowler had to spend a harrowing day to recover the empty net, injuring himself all over the body with the thorns. The quails repeated this trick whenever they were caught. The fowler's wife taunted her husband for returning empty. The fowler waited for the birds to lose their unity. One day, a few birds picked up quarrel among themselves. Noticing this, Bodhisattva thought that the time has come for him to go elsewhere. He went away with his followers. One day, again, the net was cast over the birds. They, instead of flying together, quarrelled with each other and were finally caught by the fowler.

As in the Hitopadesha, once a dove-king named Chitragriba was hovering in the sky with his retinue. A crow saw a fowler to sprinkle rice grains on the field, spread a net over these and conceal himself in a nearby bush. The doves, while flying, noticed the rice grains. But their leader Chitragriba cautioned them saying that it was unusual for the rice grains to be spread in the midst of a forest. Hence, he advised the birds not to get tempted. A few birds picked up quarrel with him and said that such risks were at every step and in spite of that they have to collect their livelihood from the earth only. The flock then descended upon the ground and were caught in the net. Chitragriba also joined them. Then as per guidance of Chitragriba, each of them caught hold of the net and flew together. They flew to the bank of the river Gandaki, where Chitragriba's friend Hiranyaka, the king of the mice lived. At the call of Chitragriba, he came out of his den. He cut the net and set all the birds free. Both the stories are similar.

3.5.3 Singha-charma Jataka *(Sīhacamma Jātaka - 189)*

Once, there lived a merchant, who used to carry his merchandise on the back of his donkey. Wherever he used to go, he used to release the donkey with a lion's skin on its body. The donkey used to graze in the fields and eat crops without any resistance, since the guards mistook it for a lion and ran away from the spot. One day, the merchant went to a village and released him as usual in the lion's skin near the rice and barley fields. The guards of the field went to the village and came back with all the villagers duly armed. They blew conches and beat the drums. The donkey, getting frightened, started braying. Now, recognizing the donkey in the lion's skin they beat him to death.

As per the Hitopadesa, a washerman named Vilasa resided in Hastinapura. He had a donkey, which became very weak carrying heavy loads all the times. The washerman used to cover him with a Tiger's skin and let him loose in a cornfield near a forest. Owners of the cornfields used to run away mistaking the donkey for a tiger. The donkey used to graze merrily and eat to his heart's content. One day, a guard covered himself with a grey blanked and watched to donkey from a distance with bow and arrows kneeling town on the field. The donkey mistook him for a female donkey and came running towards him braying. The guard could recognize that it was a donkey and not a tiger and killed him.

The 'Lion' in the Jataka has become 'Tiger' in the Panchatantra.

3.5.4 Kuti-dushaka Jataka *(Kuṭidūsaka Jātaka - 321)*

Once Bodhisattva came to life as a bird and dwelt in a tree in the Himalayas. He built a nest, which was rainproof. One day, there was a torrential rain. The bird observed that a monkey was standing beneath the tree and was shivering with cold and chattering his teeth. He told the monkey that even being a small bird he could build a nest, carrying the straws in his beaks. Rain and other natural calamity could not affect him. The monkey, being a strong-bodied animal with two hands and two legs could easily make a house so that he could live there comfortably even in the inclement weather. The monkey got angry. He felt that the bird was insulting him. As soon as the rain ceased, the monkey got up the tree and destroyed the nest. The bird flew away to safety.

As in the Hitopadesa, there was a huge tree on the bank of the river Narmada. There stayed a few birds in their nests. One day, there was an incessant downpour. The birds saw some monkeys shivering in the cold under the tree. They felt pity and told the monkeys that, although the birds did not have hands and legs, they could build their nests with their beaks. The monkeys, who were endowed with hands and legs and a strong physique, should make good shelters for themselves. Hearing this, the monkeys got angry and destroyed the nests and spoiled the eggs as soon as the rain stopped.

Both the stories are identical.

3.5.5 Sandhi-bheda jataka *(Sandhibheda Jātaka - 349)*

Once upon a time, Bodhisattva was the king of Benares. At that time, an expecting cow was left behind in a jungle by mistake by a cowherd. A lioness, who was also expecting, got friendly with the cow. In due course, the cow delivered a calf and the lioness a cub. Both the calf and the cub became friends as they grew up together. A forester noticed this strange event and reported to the king Bodhisattva. The king asked him to report again, in case he found a third animal getting into their friendship. The forester came back to the king after a few days. He reported that a jackal had been seen roaming along with the two friends. The king predicted that the jackal would create a rift between the two and they would kill each other. The king immediately started for the forest. On reaching there, they found that the corpses of the bull and the lion were lying and the jackal was eating the flesh of both the animals alternatively.

As per the Hitopadesa, a person was passing through a forest on a bullock cart. One of his bulls named Sanjibaka got injured while travelling. The traveller deserted the injured bull in the forest and went ahead with his journey. A lion named Pingalaka and two jackals named Karataka and Damanaka lived there. The bull and the lion got friendly. Both were living together happily. The jackals spoke to both of them separately and falsely complained about the animosity one harboured against the other. Both, Sanjibaka and Pingalaka became suspicious about each other's intention. The jackals were thus able to create a rift between the two animals. Each became scared of the other. Ultimately the lion killed the bull and the shrewed jackals had a great feast.

Both the stories are similar barring some minor changes.

3.6 Jataka and the Kathasaritsgara

Bararuci composed Kathasaritsagara in the post-Buddha era. Panchatantra and Hitopadesha were in existence prior to this. From this, composition, we find references of King Chandragupta Maurya and the incidents around that time. We also observe that the Kathasaritsagara mentions about Buddhists and the Jataka stories. There are clear indications that it had sourced some of the stories from the Ramayana, the Mahabharata, the Jataka, the Panchatantra and the Hitopadesha. We shall now be going through the similar stories of the Jataka and the Kathasaritsagara.

3.6.1 Chulla-Sresthi Jataka *(Cullaka-setthi Jātaka - 4)*

Once upon a time, Bodhisattva was the treasurer of the king Brahmadatta. One day, he found a dead mouse lying on the way. He predicted that, whosoever would start business with that dead mouse, would become a rich merchant in no time. A young man, on hearing this, picked it up and sold it to another merchant as feedstock for his cat. With that small amount he bought some molasses and served the same to the florists with drinking water. Gradually, he did business with wood and grass and flourished. Ultimately he did business with the merchants, who arrived there in a ship and become very rich within four months. Bodhisattva gave in his daughter married to him.

As per the Kathasaritsagara, a merchant's son Gunaddha was asked by his mother to collect the seed capital for business from a merchant named Bisakhil. When the boy went to him, he found Bisakhil scolding a boy for losing the seed capital instead of increasing the same. He showed the boy a dead mouse and said that, one could become a rich merchant even if he started trading with the dead mouse. Hearing this, Gunaddha picked up the dead mouse and came back. Seeing this, Bisakhil laughed aloud. He sold the dead mouse to another merchant for the food of his cat for a handful of peanuts. He served this powdered peanuts with drinking water to the wood-sellers. They, in return, gave him two pieces of wood each. By selling these woods, he bought more peanuts and with that he acquired more wood. Gradually, he became a wood merchant. Once due to heavy rain the prices of wood went up very high. At that time he earned a fortune by selling the wood. He became very rich. He got a mouse made of gold and gave it to the merchant Bisakhil, from whom he had taken the dead one. On hearing the story, Bisakhil was so pleased that he gave in his daughter married to him.

This story is a replica of the Jataka with minor modification.

3.6.2 Sammodamana Jataka *(Sammodamāna Jātaka - 33)*

In the ancient days, once Bodhisattva had born as a leader of thousands of quails. A fowler came with his net to catch the quails. He first imitated the note of a quail, so that they flew down on the ground and assembled together at one place. He then, cast his net over them. As already taught by their leader, the quails put their heads up through the mesh of the net and flew together in unison with the net. They got down on a thorn-brake and after entangling the net on it, escaped through the bottom. The unlucky fowler had to spend the whole day to recover the empty net. The quails repeated this trick whenever they were caught. The fowler's wife taunted her husband for returning empty. The fowler waited for the birds to lose their unity. One day, a few birds picked up quarrel among themselves. Seeing this, Bodhisattva thought that the time has come for him to go elsewhere. He went away with his followers. One day, again, the net was cast over the birds. They, instead flying together, quarrelled with each other and were caught by the fowler.

As per the Kathasaritsagara, there was a big 'Simul' tree in a forest, in which a crow named Laghupati dwelt. One day he observed from his nest that a ferocious-looking fowler was standing beneath the tree with a net and a stick. The fowler then spread his net and sprinkled handful of rice corn on the ground and hid himself in a nearby bush. At that time, Chitragriva, the king of pigeons flew down there along with his retinue to eat the rice grains and was trapped in the net. As instructed by Chitragriva, all the birds held the net with their beaks tightly and flew together. They flew with the net and landed in a field. A mouse named Hiranya, who was a friend of Chitragriva, resided there. He came out of his abode and set all the pigeons free by cutting the net with his sharp teeth.

The story is similar to the Jataka story above. There is also an identical story in the Hitopadesha, which have been narrated earlier. In this case, the resemblance with the story in Hitopadesha is more than that with the Jataka.

3.6.3 Baka Jataka *(Baka Jātaka - 38)*

A crane lived near a lotus pond full of fishes. He hit upon a plan to eat as much fish as he wished. He stood in the pond thoughtfully. When asked by the group of fishes, he told that he was worried about their welfare since the water of the pond was receding. He offered to carry them to a big lake, where they could live much better life. When they expressed their apprehension about the true intentions of the crane, the crane assured that he would not eat them. He took a big blind fish to the 'Lake' and brought him back. Actually, the fish, being blind could not see anything at all. To cover up his incapability, he cooked up an imaginary story of a "beautiful lake" and narrated the same to the others. All the fishes became eager to be shifted there. The crane carried one fish at a time in his beaks and instead of taking them to lake, took them on the branch of a tree and devoured them. In this process he ate all the fishes of the pond. Only a crab remained there. The crane also offered to transport him to the bigger lake like others. The crab doubted the integrity of the crane and wanted to be transported hanging on the crane's neck instead of the beaks. As usual, the crane started flying with him away from the lake and told that he would eat the crab as he had done to the other fishes, the crab already had this apprehension and that's why he bargained to be carried hanging on the neck. He tightened his grip on the crane's neck with his sharp claws like pincers and chopped the head off his body.

As per the Kathasaritsagara, there lived a crane near a pond. The fishes used to run away as soon as they sighted him in the pond. Thus the crane had to starve. He hit upon a plan. He told the fishes that he had information that a fisherman shall soon come to the pond for fishing and all the fishes would be caught. He also informed that there was a lake in a deserted place, unknown to the fishermen. He offered to carry the fishes there on his back. The foolish fishes believed him and agreed to his proposal. The crane started carrying the fishes on his back one by one to a rock and ate them. A crab, being suspicious asked the crane to take him to the lake, where he had taken the fishes. The crane took the crab to the rock for eating him. Seeing this, the crab cut the neck of the crane with his sharp claws and then returned to the pond and appraised the balance fishes about the whole episode.

This story has resemblance with the stories of the Jataka as well as of the Panchatantra narrated earlier.

3.6.4 Mitachinti Jataka *(Mitacinti Jātaka - 114)*

Once upon a time, there lived three fishes in a river of Benares. They were named Bahuchinti (over-thoughtful), Alpachinti (less-thoughtful) and Mitachinti (proper-thoughtful). Earlier, they had been living in the jungle areas, where no fishermen ventured. Now, they came near human-infested town, where, chances of getting caught in the net were more. Mitachinti cautioned his friends about the impending danger and requested them to go elsewhere. But the two other were enjoying stay over there since they were getting better food and were reluctant to move out. One day, foolish Bahuchinti and Alpachinti got trapped in the fishermen's net. Seeing this, Mitachinti played a trick and freed his friends.

As per the Kathasaritsagara, there lived three fishes in a lake. Their names were Anagata-bidhata, Pratyutpannamati and Yadbhavisya. One day, while passing by the lake, a few fishermen were discussing that they would be fishing in this lake. The three fishes heard this. Anagata-bidhata swam to another lake through a stream for safety. Pratyutpannamati continued to stay there with a state of high alertness and assured Yadbhavisya to help him when the need arose. When the fishermen came and started fishing, Pratyutpannamati ejected himself on ground from the water and pretended to be dead. The fishermen took him for dead started catching other Fishes. In the meantime, Pratyutpannamati jumped in the stream and swam to the other lake. Yadbhavisya was caught and killed by the fishermen.

We have noticed in the earlier chapters that this story is also present in the Mahabharata and in the Panchatantra.

3.6.5 Singha-charma Jataka *(Sīhacamma Jātaka - 189)*

Once upon a time, there lived a merchant, who used to carry his merchandise on the back of his donkey. Wherever he used to go, he used to release the donkey with a lion's skin spread on its body. The Donkey used to graze in the fields and eat crops without any resistance. Since the guards mistook it for a lion they used to ran away from the spot. One day, the merchant went to a village and released him as usual in the lion's skin near the rice and barley fields. The guards of the field went to the village and came back with all the villagers duly armed. They blew conches and beat the drums from a distance. The donkey, getting frightened, started braying. Now, recognizing the donkey in the lion's skin they beat him to death.

As in the Kathasaritsagara, a washerman used to cover his donkey with tiger's skin and release him in the cornfields. On seeing him all the people used to run away, mistaking him for a tiger. Once a farmer, who had a bow and arrows with him, saw the donkey and also mistook him for a tiger. He covered himself with a grey blanket and tried to crawl away from the field. The donkey saw him from a distance and mistook him for a female donkey and started braying.

At this, the farmer could recognize the true identity of the animal and killed him with his arrows.

This story also appears in the Hitopadesha as narrated earlier.

3.6.6 Kuranga-mriga Jataka *(Kuraṅga-miga Jātaka - 206)*

Once upon a time B dhisattva came to life as an Antelope. He used to reside in the thicket of a forest by the side of a lake. There also lived a woodpecker in a nearby tree and a tortoise in the Lake. The three were good friends. One day, a hunter laid a trap and the antelope got entangled in it. The bird and the tortoise immediately embarked upon the rescue mission. While the tortoise kept on biting the leather trap to cut it, the bird flew to the hunter's house to keep him at bay as long as possible. When the hunter came out of the front door in dawn, the bird flew towards him, flapping his wings on his face with shriek. The hunter, considering it a bad omen, went to bed for a while and started again later through the rear door. The bird repeated the act. The hunter, again, taking it for a bad omen slept till sunrise. Seeing the hunter moving thereafter, the bird went back and informed his friends. By then, the tortoise had almost cut the trap. The antelope gave a jerk with full might, freed himself and ran to a distances. The tortoise was bleeding profusely following his incessant attempt to chew the leather trap and was too weak to move out quickly. The hunter found the trap lying empty. He then discovered the tortoise lying over there. He caught hold the tortoise and put him in his bag. Seeing his, the antelope lured the hunter by standing at a safe distance. The hunter threw the bag on the ground and ran after the antelope. Having lured away the hunter to a long distance, the antelope sped back to the bag, tore it with the help of his horns and freed the turtle. Thus, getting freed, the tortoise crawled towards the lake and the dove in to the depth of the water. The antelope also sped away and vanished in the thicket of the forest. Thus they saved themselves.

As per the Kathasaritsagara, there lived four friends in a forest near a river. They were Chitranga - the deer, Mantharak - the tortoise, Laghupati - a crow and Hiranya - the mouse. One day, when Chitranga did not report at the scheduled time, Laghupati started having aerial surveillance for him from the top of a high-rise tree. He found Chitranga in a snare by the side of the river. Laghupati went back and informed Mantharak and Hiranya. He carried Hiranya to the spot in his beaks, which promptly cut the snare and freed the deer. The Tortoise Mantharak, instead of going into the river, walked towards the spot to meet the friends. At that time, the hunter arrived and found that the deer had run away. Instead, finding the turtle, he caught him, carried him in the net on his back and pursued the deer. Seeing this, on the advice of Hiranya, the deer laid at a distance pretending dead. The crow sat on its head peaking on its eye. The hunter, being delighted, left the tortoise in the net and went to catch the deer. In the meantime, the mouse cut the net and freed the tortoise, which rushed into the river. Seeing him getting freed, the deer sprang back to his feet and quickly vanished in the thicket of the forest. The crow went up the tree and the mouse hid in a hole. The hunter, losing his prized catches went empty handed blaming it on his fate.

The story also appears in the Panchatantra as already narrated. The original source seems to be the Jataka, from where, the transformed version appears in the Panchatantra and further revised in the Kathasaritsagara.

3.6.7 Sisumara Jataka *(Sumsumāra Jātaka - 208)* Vanara Jataka *(Vānara Jātaka - 342)*

In these Jatakas, Bodhisattva had born as a monkey and used to live in a forest adjacent to the river Ganges on the foothills of the *Himalayas.* He grew strong and sturdy and lived on the fruits of the trees those grew on the bank of the river. A crocodile couple lived in the river. The female crocodile expressed to her mate that she longed to eat the heart of a monkey. The crocodile planned to catch the monkey. He told the monkey that verities of fruits were available on the other side of the river. The monkey expressed his inability to swim. The crocodile offered to ferry him on his back. The monkey believing the crocodile sailed on his back. After a while, the crocodile started sinking. On inquiry, the crocodile replied that he was taking him to his under-water home as his mate wanted to eat his heart. The Monkey promptly replied, "We keep our hearts on the fig trees, otherwise, while jumping from one tree to another, these would be knocked down to pieces". Then, pointing to a fig tree, he asked the crocodile to take him there, so that he could pluck the heart from the tree and gave the same for his friend's wife. The crocodile took him to the shore. The monkey leapt off his back on a tree and exclaimed that the crocodile was indeed a great fool.

As per the Kathasaritsagara, a monkey king named Baliraj being separated from his troop used to reside on a fig tree on seashore. One day, a ripe fig slipped from his hands and fell into the sea, which was eaten by a crocodile. The crocodile liked the taste of the fig and everyday used to come to the shore and requested the monkey to throw a few pieces. The monkey obliged him. Gradually, a friendship developed between the two and the crocodile used to spend the whole day with his friend. Knowing this, the crocodile's wife feigned illness and longed to eat the heart of a monkey. The crocodile did not like to kill his friend but considering the choice between the lives of his wife and his friend, he decided to kill the monkey. Next day, he lured the monkey to go to his house on his back. The unsuspecting monkey gladly agreed and sailed on his friend's back towards his abode. The crocodile gradually started sinking in the water. When the frightened monkey enquired, the crocodile divulged that he was being taken as his heart can alone save the crocodile's wife from the certain death. On hearing this, the monkey said that his heart was kept in the tree. The stupid crocodile believed this and sailed him back ashore near the tree. The monkey leapt back onto the tree and said that the crocodile was a real fool.

The story also appears in the Panchatantra. It seems that Jataka had been the source for this story for both the Pañchatantra as well as the Kathasaritsagara.

3.6.8 Kachhapa Jataka *(Kacchapa Jātaka - (215)*

Once upon a time, a tortoise dwelt in a lake in the Himalayan region. He grew friendship with two wild geese. One day, the geese decided to take their friend tortoise to the beautiful abode at the Chitrakut plateau. Both the geese held a stick in their beaks. The turtle hung biting the stick from the middle. Before flying, they cautioned the tortoise not to open his mouth under any circumstances. While they were flying above the locality, boys on the ground below them started telling each other about the unprecedented event. Hearing this, the tortoise got angry and he tried to scold the boys. As soon as he opened his mouth, he fell on the ground and split into two halves.

As per the Kathasaritsagara, there lived a tortoise named Kambugriva in a lake. He had two geese friends named Vikata and Sankata. One day, the lake almost dried up as a result of severe drought. The geese planned to go to another lake and settle there. The tortoise requested them to take him also there. The geese asked him to bite a stick strongly and not to open his mouth under any circumstances. They caught hold of both the ends of the stick with their beaks and flew with their friend. While flying, the people below started shouting seeing this unprecedented scene. The curious turtle opened his mouth to enquire about the noise. He fell on the ground immediately and was killed by the inhabitants.

We find an identical story in the Panchatantra as narrated earlier. This is another case, where all the stories seem to have originated from the Jataka.

3.6.9 Kuta-banijya Jataka *(Kūṭa-vāṇija Jātaka - 218)*

Once upon a time, two traders, one from a village and the other from a town were friends. Once, the trader from the village came to his friend in the town and kept five hundred ploughshares with him. He said that he would be back after a long time. As soon as his friend went away, the townsman sold these and kept the money with him. He them sprinkled some mouse-dung in the storage space. When the villager returned and asked for the ploughshares, the friend showed him the space filled with the mouse-dung and said that the mice had eaten the ploughshares.

The villager although understood everything, did not utter a single word. He took the son of the townsman with him and said that he was going to the river for bathing. But instead of going to the river, he went to another friend's house and kept his friend's son there. He then returned to the townsman and reported that a hawk had carried away his son from the riverbank. The townsman did not believe this and took his friend to the Court of justice. The Judge asked as to how a hawk could carry away a grown up boy. The villager replied that if the mice could eat the ploughshares, why not a hawk could carry away his friend's son. On enquiry by the Judge, he narrated the story to the Judge. The Judge ordered the townsman to return the ploughshares and villager the boy. They did accordingly and the case got settled.

As per the Kathasaritsagara, there lived a merchant's son, who inherited only an Iron Balance weighing 50 Seers (100 Pounds). He kept it with his merchant friend and went outstations. When he returned and asked for his balance, the friend said that the rats had eaten it up. The merchant understood the story, smiled and asked his friend not to bother for this. He then wanted to have his lunch there, to which, his friend readily agreed. He went to take bath in the river with his friend's son. After having bath, he hid the child in the house of another friend and returned. On return, he informed his friend that a hawk had carried away his son. The merchant got angry at this and took his friend to the Court of justice. On inquiry by the Judge, the merchant said if the mice could eat the iron balance, it should not appear impossible for a hawk to take away a boy. Hearing this, the Judge understood the background story and ordered both the merchants to return each other's belongings. They did so and the case got settled.

An identical story also appears in the Panchatantra as narrated earlier. Both the stories in the Kathasaritsagara and the Panchatantra seem to own their origins from the Jataka.

3.6.10 Uluka Jataka *(Ulūkā Jātaka - 270)*

Once, in the primitive age, each type of living beings gathered together and selected their leaders. Human beings selected a handsome, auspicious and commanding man as their king. The quadrupeds chose lion as their leader. The fishes selected a fish named Ananda as the king. Likewise, the birds also assembled and elected the owl as the leader. The crow raised objection. He said, if our king's face looked so ugly when he is pleased, one could imagine as to how would he look when he were angry. He further declared that he did not accept the owl as his king and flew away. At this, the owl got angry and chased the crow. The birds nominated the golden goose as their king. Thenceforth, there had been an animosity between the crow and the owl.

As per the Kathasaritsagara, in the ancient days, the birds did not have a king. They flocked together and chose owl as their leader. The crow objected to this saying that the owl was ugly, inauspicious, cruel-looking and blind during the day and as such did not possess any quality to become the king of the birds. Hearing this, they cancelled the appointment of the owl and went back to their respective nests. Thereafter, an animosity grew between the owl and the crow.

The story of the Kathasaritsagara is almost a replica of the Jataka story.

3.6.11 Sandhi-bheda Jataka *(Sandhibheda Jātaka - 349)*

Once upon a time, Bodhisattva was the king of Benares. At that time, an expecting cow was left behind in a jungle mistakenly by a cowherd. The cow got friendly with a lioness, who was also expecting. In due course, the cow delivered a calf and the lioness a cub. Both the calf and the cub became friends as they grew up together. A Forester noticed this strange event and reported to the king Bodhisattva. The king asked him to report again, in case he found a third animal getting into their friendship. After a few days, the forester came back to the king. He reported that a jackal had been seen roaming along with the two friends. The king predicted that the jackal would create a rift between the two friends and they would kill each other. The king started for the forest. On reaching there, they found that the corpses of the bull and the lion were lying there and the jackal was devouring the flesh of both the animals alternatively.

As per the Kathasaritsagara, once a person was travelling through a forest. One of his bulls named Sanjivaka got hurt in one of his legs. He was unable to walk normally. The master deserted the injured bull in the forest and proceeded further in his journey. A lion named Pinganaka and two Jackals named Karataka and Damanaka lived in that forest. The bull and the lion got friendly. The jackals created a rift between the two by instigating the two friends against each other. Each of them started doubting the intentions of the other. Ultimately, the lion killed the bull and the sly jackals had lavish meals.

Hitopadesa also have an identical story in which the name of the lion has been mentioned as Pingalaka.

3.6.12 Unmadayanti Jataka *(Ummadanti Jātaka - 527)*

Once upon a time, Bodhisattva had born to the queen-consort of king Sivi in the kingdom of Sivi. At the same time, a son was also born to the king's Commander-in-Chief and was named as Ahiparaka. Both the boys grew up and were educated together. In due course, prince Sivi ascended the throne and became king Sivi. Ahiparaka became his Commander-in-Chief. In the same city dwelt a merchant named Tiritavachha, who had a daughter named Unmadayanti. She was extremely beautiful and was fit for any king. The merchant proposed his daughter's marriage with the king. The king sent four Brahmins to the merchant's house to ascertain whether the girl was fit for him. The Brahmins went to the merchant's house. On seeing the beauty of Unmadayanti they got so intoxicated that they lost self control and started behaving abnormally. At this, Unmadayanti got annoyed and drove the Brahmins out of her house. They felt insulted but they were not in a position to tell the truth to the king. To hush up the matter, they reported to the king that the girl was not suitable for him. Unmadayanti later got married to Ahiparaka. On the day of 'Kartika festival', the king went round the city and happened to see the surpassing beauty of Unmadayanti. He got maddened in the passion for her. When Ahiparaka came to know about this, he offered his wife to the king. But the king ultimately controlled himself and gradually overcame the craze for Unmadayanti.

As per the Kathasaritsagara, a king named Devasena reigned in the kingdom. A very rich merchant used to reside there. He had an exceptionally beautiful daughter named Unmadini (*Ummadantī* in *Pāli*). He proposed to the king for marriage of this daughter with him. The king sent four Brahmins to assess the suitability of the girl to become his queen. The Brahmins were surprised to see her over-charming beauty. They thought that if the king were married to this girl, he may forget his official task altogether and get immersed in deep love with the queen. They told the king that the girl was not suitable for him. Unmadini got married to the commander-in-chief of the king. The king happened to see her in course of time and got struck by extreme passion for her. Upon knowing this, the Commander-in-Chief offered his wife to the king but the good-natured king did not accept the offer. Gradually, the king died in the passion for her.

The story of the Kathasaritsagara is a replica of the Jataka story.

4.0 JATAKA AND ANCIENT FOREIGN LITERATURE

GREAT GREEK POET HOMER

4.1 Jataka and the Odyssey

As per the Greek belief, the great minstrel Homer verbally composed Iliad and Odyssey. He used to sing the heroic deeds of the past great Greek warriors. Homer is dated back to 750-700 BC and was an inhabitant of Ionia, the Greek-inhabited coast and island off west-central Turkey. The origin of the Odyssey is traced back to the 13th Century BC, when the great Trojan War is said to have taken place. Since then, the oral poets used to sing the heroic deeds of the Greek heroes. Homer had compiled these in 12000 lines. Some historians opined that, these epics could have even been written in around 700 BC. Homer may have composed the oral traditional lyrics in proper style. The epic revolves around the story of heroic expedition of a Greek King of Ithaca named Odysseus. He set out for the famous War of Troy and returned home after twenty long years. It took nine years to end the Trojan War. Thereafter, he set back for his home and that story is portrayed in the Odyssey. We shall now go through those parts of the stories, which are similar to the Jataka and the Odyssey.

4.1.1 Losaka Jataka *(Losaka-Jātaka - 41)* Mitravinda Jataka *(Mittavinda-Jātaka - 82)*

Once upon a time, a Buddhist Brother was living in a village and was maintained well by the landlord. One day, another Brother reached there and was also well-treated by the landlord. This made the former Brother jealous and he ill-treated the newcomer. As a result, the jealous Brother had to take many rebirths and also had to undergo tremendous misery. After many rebirths as Yaksha and Dog, he had reborn again as a human being. His name was Mitravindaka. Wherever he used to stay, his neighbours had to face the nature's wrath because of his association and ultimately used to drive him out. One day, he boarded a ship as an employee of that ship. After seven days of smooth sailing, the ship became standstill in the mid-ocean. The sailors came to know through throw of lot that this was due to the inauspicious association of Mitravindaka. They deserted him in the sea on a bamboo-raft. Mitravindaka sailed in the raft and found divine maidens in the crystal palaces in the sea. He spent time merrily with them. He was not satisfied and desired to have more fun. He sailed further and landed in the city of Ogress. He found a goat, which was actually an Ogress. He tried to catch her to make a meal of her. The goat kicked him so vigorously that he landed in Benares. There, he found the king's goats grazing in a field. He thought that he could get back to the crystal palaces in the sea, where the divine maidens dwelt. To get a similar kick, he held the leg of a goat. The goatherds ran in and seized him mistaking him for a goat-thief. While he was being taken to the king for punishment, Bodhisattva met him on the way and freed him.

LAESTRYGONIANS THROWING HEAVY ROCKS ON ODYSSEUS' SHIPS.

4.1.2 Mitravinda Jataka *(Mittavinada Jātaka - 104)* Mitravinda Jataka *(Mittavinada Jātaka - 369)* Chatu-dwara Jataka *(Catu-dvāra Jātaka - 439)*

These tales have slight variations to the tale narrated above. Here, Mitravindaka is depicted as the son of a merchant having immense wealth. After the death of his father, he ill-treated his mother, bought a ship and sailed on the same. The ship got stranded in the mid-sea after seven days of smooth sailing and Mitravindaka was deserted on a Bamboo-raft as in the previous story. He sailed further and reached crystal palaces, where he spent pleasant days in the company of the divine maidens. Thereafter, he sailed further in the search for more luck. Ultimately, he reached the *Ussada* Hell. He found there a person holding a razor-wheel over his head and doing penance for his evil deeds. Mitravindaka mistook it for a Lotus bloom and thought that he could became the king of this lovely kingdom once he could snatch it away from the person and held it over his own head. He did so. The man on getting relieved ran away to freedom. The wheel got fixed on Mitravindaka's head. He then realized that the wheel was a razor-wheel, meant to punish the guilty. Bodhisattva happened to visit the *Ussada* hell, when he found Mitravindaka holding the razor-wheel. He explained Mitravindaka the reasons for his punishment.

We shall now visit the story of the Odyssey. Odysseus, the king of Ithaca, set sail for home after ten years on the end of the War of Troy. On the way, the ships were caught in a heavy storm and typhoon. It became out of control of the sailors and went in unknown direction. On the tenth day they reached ashore. Odysseus sent three persons to the land to survey about its inhabitants. There grew a sweet fruit in this country called Lotus. The inhabitants offered the Lotus fruit to the sailors. On taking these, they fell asleep. Odysseus went in search of them and found them sleeping. Due to the reaction of the lotus fruits, the sailors were not at all willing to leave the country. They were forcibly taken to the ship. The ships sailed away from there.

The ships reached the country of Cyclops. There were many wild goats grazing without fear. The sailors caught hold of many goats and slaughtered them for food. Odysseus went to the land with a few associates. There, they went to a cave, where a giant one-eyed Cyclops named Polyphemus lived. Odysseus and his associates were held captive by the demon. He ate some of the men. Odysseus and the rest of the men blinded him with a sharp olive pole and escaped in the ship.

The ships sailed again. After a few days, they were drifted by stormy weather to some unknown direction. The ships reached a floating island named Aeolia, the home of the god of winds, named Aeolus. All round the island ran a high wall of Bronze. Aeolus had given his six daughters married to his six sons. All of them lived luxuriously always feasting with countless delicacies. Aeolus welcomed Odysseus and his men and entertained them for a whole month. He made arrangements for their further voyage. He presented Odysseus with a leather bag, in which, he had imprisoned the boisterous energies of all the winds. He warned Odysseus not to open it, lest the imprisoned storm wrecked havoc on their voyage. He then ordered the cool breeze to sail the ships safely to their homeland. After nine days of smooth sailing, they almost reached Ithaca, when Odysseus felt fast asleep due to fatigue. The sailors thought that the leather bag contained valuables. They wanted to share those amongst themselves. As soon as they opened the bag, storm rose and dragged the ships back to Aeolia. Aeolus got angry with Odysseus and his men and drove them out of his island immediately.

They had to sail again in the rough weather. After six days they reached Telepylus. They anchored the ships there and sent three men ashore to investigate about the country. They found a cart road and a girl. The girl was the daughter of Antiphates, the Laestrygonian chief. When the men enquired from her regarding the ruler of the country, she showed them the house of her father. Antiphates and his wife were giants. Antiphates caught a sailor and ate him like eating a carrot. The other two ran for their lives and boarded the ships.

Meanwhile, the Laestrygonians came to the cliff by the side of the sea and started showering heavy rocks on the ships. They killed sailors and broke all the ships excepting the Odysseus' one, which was anchored away in the sea. Odysseus' ship sailed away very fast to the deep sea again.

In due course, the ship came to the island of Aeaea, the home of beautiful Circe, a formidable goddess. She was the sister of the beautiful Aeetes and both were the children of the Sun. On reaching the shore, the sailors lay on the beach for two days. On the third day, Odysseus tried to gaze the place from a rock and found smoke bellowing out at a distant place. On his way back to the ship, he killed a huge stag and carried it to the ship for meals. He divided the sailors in two groups of 22 each. He and Eurylochus took charge of the two groups. Eurylochus and his 22 men went to Circe's house built with polished stones. Prowling around the palace were mountain wolves and lions bewitched by Circe through her magic drugs. They did not harm any man. Circe welcomed the people. All the men went inside. Only Eurylochus stayed outside to watch. The men inside were offered food and drink and were converted into pigs by Circe through her magic. Eurylochus returned to the ship and narrated the story to Odysseus. Odysseus alone set for Circe's house with his Silver-Bronze sword and bow. On the way, Hermes, the god of golden wand appeared and gave him an herb, which he said, would act as an antidote against Circe's black magic. Odysseus went to Circe's house and was welcomed by her. With the herb given by Hermes, Odysseus freed his men form Circe's clutch and had unlimited fun with her. He spent one whole year in Circe's warm hospitality with his men.

After a year, they sailed for Ithaca via the Hall of Hades as advised by Circe. The Hall of Hades was the place where all the dead persons lived. Odysseus met there his ex-comrade Elpenor, mother Anticleia, King Agamemnon, lord Teiresias and many others. Teiresias foretold him the future and gave directions for going back to Ithaca. The ship returned again to the island of Aeaea. They spent another day and night in Circe's warmth. Circe gave advice to Odysseus regarding the return journey.

As advised by Circe, Odysseus poured bee-wax in the ears of the sailors before crossing the Sirens' island. He ordered the sailors to tie him up right on the top of the mast. While crossing the island, he could listen to the melodious songs of Sirens but did not encounter any problem due to the precautions already taken.

No sooner they rowed past the island, they saw a cloud of spume ahead and raging surf and heard thunders of breakers. They had to sail through a strait, on one side of which lived a rock demon Scylla and on the other side the awesome Charybdis. While crossing the strait, six sailors were lifted from the ship by Scylla and eaten.

Soon, they reached the Sun god's lovely isle. It was full of flocks of splendid sturdy sheep of the Sun god. Odysseus categorically warned his people not to harm any sheep. In spite of Odysseus' warning, his men slaughtered a sheep for meals. Fearing problem, they set sail immediately. During the night, the ship was caught in the worst thunderstorm. The ship broke into fragments. All the sailors died excepting Odysseus, who kept himself afloat by holding a broken mast.

After floating for nine days, he was thrown on an isle named Ogygia, inhibited by a nymph named Calypso. Odysseus had to spend seven long years in the company of Calypso. She wanted to marry Odysseus and stay with him forever. But as per wish of the gods, she made arrangements for his return voyage to Ithaca. Odysseus made a boat and sailed. This boat also sank and he was drifted ashore to the country of Phaeacians. He met the princess Nausicaa in totally battered and naked condition. Nausicaa bathed him and took him to his father Alcinous' palace. Alcinous welcomed him, gave lot of gifts and sends him to Ithaca in a ship. The sailors left him ashore Ithaca with all the boxes of gifts. Odysseus thus reached him homeland after a long period.

4.1.3 Balahassa Jataka *(Valāhassa Jātaka - 196)*

Once upon a time, there was a town in the island of Ceylon, called Sirisavasthu. The town was infested by she-goblins. Wherever a ship wrecked, they used to lure the sailors to their huts, marry and live with them and finally ate them. Once, a ship wrecked. The she-goblins lured the five hundred traders and made them their husbands. One day, the chief trader could realize that these ladies were goblins. He asked his entire fellow traders to quit the island immediately. While, two hundred fifty Traders prepared to leave, the others preferred to stay and enjoy. Bodhisattva arrived there in the form of a winged horse and carried these people to their respective homes. The others, who stayed back were slaughtered by the goblins in due course and eaten.

As per the Odyssey, there was an island infested by "Sirens". The Sirens were beautiful ladies, whose melodious voice used to bewitch the sailors. The sailors passing by the island used to get attracted by the clear and loud songs of the Sirens and used to loose their lives when landed on the island. The Sirens used to sit on their skeletons in the meadows and sang. As advised by the goddess Circe, Odysseus poured bee wax in the ears of the sailors, got himself tied up to the mast and sailed past the isle of Sirens unharmed.

From the foregoing, we find that there are some shadow resemblances between the stories of the Jataka and the Odyssey. We have observed in the beginning that the Odyssey was orally composed during the 13th century BC and finally composed by Homer in the refined form in the 700 BC, whilst, the Jataka stories came into being only after the birth of the Buddha i.e. well after 550 BC. Hence, the resemblances, if any, could be logically attributed to the older story of the Odyssey.

AESOP

4.2 Jataka and Aesop's Fables

As per the legend, Aesop was born in the 620 BC and died in 560 BC. He was contemporary of Lord Buddha, who survived from 624BC to 544BC. Aesop is said to have born either in Sardis, situated on the Greek island of Samos or in Cotiaeum, the chief city in a province of Phrygian. Aesop was enslaved and was the property of a citizen named Iadmon, who resided in the island of Somas. Impressed by Aesop's wisdom and wits, which helped Iadmon settle ugly disputes, he granted freedom to Aesop. As a free man, he is thought to have travelled to Athens, where he became a crusader against injustice and a saviour of the common people. His fame spread quickly and he was loved and respected by the common people. Peisistratus, the notorious ruler of Athens, who was a fierce enemy to the freedom of speech, obviously did not like this. In 560 BC, Aesop was condemned to death for sacrilege by the infamous oracle of Delphi and was thrown over a cliff at Hypania. The noble fables survived even after the death of Aesop and were compiled by the Greek scholars later in the Alexandria Library under the title, "Assemblies of Aesopic Tales". Thus, the first edition of the collection came into being in 300 BC in a free speech Greek society. How many of these two hundred and odd Fables were really authored by Aesop could not be established authentically. However, it is told that the fables from Libya and India also added to the present collection of Aesop's Fables. We shall be reading the common stories between the Aesop's Fables and the Jataka.

4.2.1 Munika Jataka *(Muṇika Jātaka - 30)* Saluka Jataka *(Sālūka Jātaka - 286)*

Once upon a time, Bodhisattva had born as an ox and

was named Mahalohita. His brother's name was Chullalohita. Both of them used to stay in a farmer's house in a certain hamlet. They used to do all hard work and used to get grass and straw as their food. One day, the farmer bought a pig, which was being fed with all rich foods and it got healthier day by day. Seeing this, Chullalohita told his elder brother that although they did all hard work, they were kept on ordinary diet, whereas the pig, without doing any work gets plentiful of delicious foods. Mahalohita consoled his brother and asked him not to repent on his fate. In a few days' time, the farmer's daughter's marriage ceremony was held. The pig was butchered on the occasion for the feast. Seeing this, Chullalohita stopped repenting.

In the Munika Jataka, the name of the pig was Munika, whereas the same was Saluka in the other Jataka.

The Aesop's Fables carries a story titled, "The Heifer and the Ox," which is similar to the above story. A Heifer that ran wild in the fields and had never felt the yoke derided an ox at plough for submitting himself to such labour and drudgery. The ox said nothing but went on with his work. Not long after the incident, there was a festival. The ox was granted a holiday, but the heifer was led off to be sacrificed at the altar. "If this is the rewards for your idleness", the ox said, "Then I think my work is more rewarding than your play. Indeed, I'd rather have my neck feel the yoke than the axe".

4.2.2 Benuka Jataka *(Veḷuka Jātaka - 43)*

Once upon a time, *Bodhisattva* used to live in a hermitage in the *Himalayas* as an ascetic with five hundred followers. One day, a young poisonous snake came wondering to the hut of a Brother, who started rearing it in a bamboo cage as his own son. When Bodhisattva came to know about it, he warned the Brother of the imminent danger and asked him to refrain from this. The Brother was not convinced and continued to do the same. One day, the Brother, along with others had gone to the forest to fetch some fruits. The snake became angry due to hunger. When the Brother returned, he went to fondle and feed the snake. The Snake bit his foster father to death and escaped to the jungle.

The above story is similar to the story of the Aesop's Fable titled "The Farmer and the Snake" which goes as follows. While returning home on a winter day, a farmer found a snake lying under a hedge, half dead with cold. Taking pity on the creature, he placed it in his bosom and brought it home, where he laid it upon the hearth near the fire. No sooner was the snake restored to normalcy by the warmth of the cottage than it began to attack the farmer's wife and children. Hearing their cries, the farmer, whose compassion had saved the snake's life, rushed into the room, grabbed an axe, and kept on hitting the serpent until it was dead.

4.2.3 Birala Jataka *(Bilāra Jātaka - 128)*

In this Jataka, Bodhisattva had born as the leader of hundreds of rats. The rats went in a troop every morning in search of food and returned in the evening together. A jackal hit upon a plan to eat the rats. One morning, he took position near the rats' den standing on one leg facing the Sun. He kept his mouth open and kept on snuffing air. When asked by the leader of the rats, he explained that he was looking towards the Sun to worship him, standing on one leg to reduce his burden on the earth and was inhaling air since this was his only food. Mistaking him to be of saintly nature they believed him and did not consider him an enemy any more. From next day onwards, the jackal used to stand the same way but used to catch the hindmost rat and eat it. The count of the rats gradually dwindled. Doubting the jackal's saintliness, one day Bodhisattva remained on the hindmost position of the troop. The jackal, as usual, pounced upon him and tried to devour him. Bodhisattva, along with other rats attacked the jackal and killed him.

4.2.4 Agnika Jataka *(Aggika Jātaka - 129)*

In this Jataka also Bodhisattva had born as the king of rats. A jackal, which was trapped in a jungle fire, lost all hair on his body in the flame, leaving a tuff on his crown, similar to one, kept by some saints. He looked different to other jackals and offered his services as a supervisor to the rat brethren. The rats, taking him for a saint, agreed to this. The jackal used to devour the hindmost rat as detailed in the previous story. Discovering this, the rat-king Bodhisattva drove him away.

There is a matching story to the above Jatakas in the Aesop's Fables titled, "The Wolf and the Shepherd". A wolf followed a flock of sheep for a long time and made no attempt to attack them. However, the shepherd had his suspicions, and for a while he was always on the guard against him. But when the wolf stayed close to the flock days after days without trying to seize any one of them, he began to regard him more as a friend rather than a foe. One day, when he had to go to the town, he decided to entrust the sheep to his care. However, no sooner did the shepherd left for the town, than the wolf fell upon the flock of the sheep and devoured them. Upon his return, the shepherd could found nothing else but the remains of his flock.

4.2.5 Subarna-hamsa Jataka *(SuvaKKahamsa Jātaka (136)*

Once upon a time, Bodhisattva took birth as a Brahmin householder. He married a lady and had three daughters. One day he died. He had reborn as a golden mallard with full consciousness of his previous birth and family. He came to see his wife and daughters, who had taken up the jobs of maids after his death. The mallard used to give one golden feather to his family every day, so that; they could live happily without having to work as maids in the neighbourhood. Bodhisattva's ex-wife became greedy. One day she plucked all the feathers from the body of the mallard at a time to become rich instantaneously. All gold feathers turned into ordinary white feathers. The mallard was in terrible pains and could not fly. In due course of time the feathers grew again. As soon as he could, he flew away and never returned again.

The story of the Aesop's Fables titled, "The Goose with the Golden Eggs" is as follows. Once, there was a man, who was lucky to own a goose, who laid him a golden egg every day. By selling these, he could earn a great fortune. Gradually he became greedy. He wanted to become very rich overnight. Since the process of getting rich was slow, he eventually killed the goose. After cutting open her body, he found that there was nothing dissimilar to a normal goose. He could never get the golden eggs again.

4.2.6 Virochana Jataka *(Virocana Jātaka - 143)* Jambuka Jataka *(Jambuka Jātaka - 335)*

Once Bodhisattva had born as a mighty lion and used to live on the meat of the large animals he killed. One day he killed a buffalo and was returning to his cave after eating its flesh. On the way a jackal appeared, who pleaded to become his servant. The lion granted his prayer.

Thenceforth, the lion used to kill big animals and ate the flesh and the jackal also used to get the residue as his share. The jackal, in due course, became jealous of the lion and thought that he could also kill big animals like his master. He felt that he was in no way inferior to the lion. In spite of repeated warnings of the lion, he decided to kill an elephant as the lion usually did. One day, he found an elephant coming towards him. He howled thrice like the lion and jumped before the Elephant. The Elephant crushed the jackal with his forefoot.

The story of the Aesop's Fables, "The Lion and the Fox" is almost similar to the Jataka story and is as under.

A fox agreed to work for a lion as a servant, and for a while, each carried out his respective duties according to his own nature and powers. The Fox used to search for and point out the prey. The lion would attack and seize it. The fox, however, soon became jealous of the lion as the lion used to get lion's share of the prey. The fox thought that, he was just as good as his master. He declared that he would no longer simply discover the prey but capture it on his own. The next day, he attempted to snatch a lamb from the fold of a hunter like the lion. The hunter and his hounds pounced on him and killed him on the spot.

4.2.7 Singha-Charma Jataka *(Sīhacamma Jātaka - 189)*

Once, there lived a merchant, who used to carry his merchandise on the back of his donkey. Wherever he used to go, he used to release the donkey with a lion's skin on it. The donkey used to graze in the fields and eat crops without any resistance. The guards mistook it for a lion and used to run away from the spot. One day, the merchant went to a village and released him as usual in the lion's skin near the rice and barley fields. The guard of the field mistook it for a lion. He went to the village and came back with all the villagers duly armed. They blew conches and beat the drums. The donkey, getting frightened, started braying. Now, recognizing the donkey in the lion's skin, they beat him to death.

The story titled "The Ass in the Lion's skin" of the Aesop's Fables is the replica of the Jataka story. The story is as follows.

After putting on a lion's skin, an ass roamed around freely and amused himself by frightening all the foolish animals he encountered. Upon meeting a fox, he tried to scare him as well. Incidentally, the jackal happened to hear his voice. He said, "I would have been frightened too, but your braying gave you away".

4.2.8 Kachhapa Jataka *(Kacchapa Jātaka - 215)*

Once, a tortoise dwelt in a lake in the Himalayan region. He grew friendship with two wild geese. One day, the geese decided to take their tortoise friend to their abode at the beautiful Chitrakut plateau. Both the geese held the end of a stick in their beaks. The turtle hung biting the stick in the middle. Before flying, the geese asked the tortoise not to open his mouth under any circumstances. While they were overflying a locality, boys on the ground below started talking loudly about the unprecedented event. Hearing this, the tortoise got angry and he tried to scold the boys. As soon as he opened his mouth, he fell on the ground and split into two halves.

This story is similar to the story in the Aesop's Fables titled, "The Tortoise and the Eagle", which goes as follows.

A tortoise was dissatisfied with his lowly life and with the crawling about on the ground at a snail's pace. He envied the birds and wanted to soar high into the clouds.

He thought, once he was in the air, he could also fly like them. So one day he offered an Eagle all the treasures in the ocean if he would teach him how to fly. The Eagle declined and told that a tortoise's desire to fly was not only absurd but was impossible. However, the tortoise could not be desisted from his ambition to fly. He kept on insisting and pleading to the eagle. Under intense pressure, the eagle had to agree to fulfil the turtle's desire. He, therefore, carried the tortoise to the high air on his back, relieved him off him body and asked him to spread his legs like the wings of a bird. But, before the tortoise could do anything, he plunged straight down, hit a rock and split into pieces.

THE FOX AND THE CROW

4.2.9 Jambu-khadaka Jataka (*Jambu-Khādaka Jātaka - 294)*

Once a crow, perched upon a rose apple tree was eating the ripe fruit delightfully. A jackal came beneath the tree and longed for the fruits, which were out of bound for him. The jackal started flattering the crow. He praised its beauty, voice etc. The crow became very pleased and also flattered the jackal in a similar fashion. He further dropped some ripe fruits for the jackal to eat. Jackal's trick worked and he could enjoy the delicious fruits, which were otherwise beyond his reach.

4.2.10 Anta Jataka (*Anta Jātaka - 295)*

Once, the carcass of an old dead ox was dumped on the outskirts of a village under a castor oil tree. A jackal came and started feasting on the carcass. Meanwhile, a crow longed for the rotten flesh of the carcass. He started flattering the jackal, who became very proud of himself and started complementing the crow in return. He also invited the crow to have an unlimited and delicious lunch with him on the carcass.

A similar tale to the above Jataka stories is found in the Aesop's Fables titled, "The Fox and the Crow". In this, a crow stole a large piece of cheese from a household and perched over a tree to enjoy it. A jackal, standing beneath the tree wanted to grab the same. He started praising the beauty of the crow. The crow, to impress the jackal with his voice began to caw. The cheese fell from his beaks and the sly fox snapped it up and quickly. The jackal also said that the crow was a real fool.

THE WOLF AND THE CRANE

4.2.11 Jabasakuna Jataka *(Javasakuṇa Jātaka - 308)*

Once, Bodhisattva had born in a forest as a woodpecker. A lion also dwelt in the same forest. One day, a bone got stuck to the throat of the lion while devouring his prey. The lion was in extreme discomfort and pain. He requested the woodpecker to remove the bone and he promised the bird a reward for his job. The woodpecker placed a piece of wooden piece between the jaws of the lion and then removed the bone from the lion's throat by inserting its beak. After removing the bone, he flicked the wooden piece and flew away to a safe distance on the branch of a tree. Later on, he asked for the reward. The lion said that the woodpecker's being able to save his head from the jaws of a Lion itself was the greatest prize.

The story of "The Wolf and the Crane" in the Aesop's Fables is a replica of the above story.

A wolf devoured his prey so ravenously that a bone got stuck to his throat. In the extreme agony he ran and howled throughout the forest. He pleaded with every animal to pull out the bone. He also declared to award a prize to one, who could cure him. All the animals and birds avoided going near him to help him. At last, a crane came forward and with its long beaks removed the bone. When he asked for the reward, the wolf just grinned and bared his teeth. He said that the crane should feel highly rewarded as he could draw out his head to safety form the jaws of a wolf.

4.2.12 Kukkuta Jataka (*Kukkuṭa Jātaka - 383*)

Once, Bodhisattva came to life as a cock. A cat, who used to kill and eat the hens, tried to lure the cock to her fold. She praised the beauty and voice of the cock and proposed to marry him. The cock refused to accept such an offer and did not get into the cat's trap.

In the Aesop's Fables, there is a story titled, "The Dog, the Cock and the Fox", which matches the above story with some deviations. In this tale, a cock and a dog were friends. They set out through a forest. When the dusk set in, the dog retired at the foot of a big tree. The cock perched himself atop the same tree. As habituated, the cock cawed loudly, which drew the attention of a sly fox. The fox flattered the cock. He said that the cock possessed a golden voice. He offered to sing and dance together, once the cock came down. The cock informed that his sacristan was at the foot of the same tree and asked the Jackal to ask him to toll the bell. The jackal, as soon as reached the foot of the tree, was killed by the dog.

4.2.13 Dhumkari Jataka (*Dhūmkāri Jātaka - 413*)

There lived a Brahmin goatherd named *Dhumkari*, who used to take care of his goats and lived happily. On a severe cold day in the winter, a herd of beautiful golden deer came there to take shelter where the goats lived. The goatherd liked the charming herd of deer. Instead of caring for his goats, he started taking care of the herd of deer. When the autumn set in, the deer ran away and vanished in the Himalayas. The goats had already died due to negligence on part of their master. Ultimately the goatherd lost everyone.

As per "The Goatherd and the Goats" of the Aesop's Fables, on a snowy and stormy day, a goatherd drove his goats in a deserted cave in a forest. Already a herd of wild goats had taken shelter there. The wild goats were much more in number and were larger in shape than the existing flock. The goatherd decided to rear the wild goats in place of his old ones. He fed the wild goats whatever food he had. When the weather cleaned up, the wild goats ran away form the shelter and his own goats had already died due to hunger. The goatherd thus lost everything.

THE WOLF AND THE LAMB

4.2.14 Dipi Jataka *(Dīpi Jātaka - 426)*

A she-goat got isolated from her herd and was left behind. She found a panther waiting on her way in the hilly terrain. Finding no other way the she-goat called the panther uncle and tried to soften his heart. The panther complained that the goat had trod upon his tail and this inflicted injury to him. The goat replied that the tail of an animal was only on the rear. Since both of them stood face to face, there was no chance for her to touch the panther's tail. The panther said that his tail was a huge one and she certainly has caused injury to the same while coming. When the she-goat said that she came by flying and as such, there was no reason to cause injury to the panther's tail. The panther said, while the goat was flying, the flock of deer ran away in fear. By this act, the goat had spoiled the meal of the panther. He accused her of spoiling his meals and finally devoured the goat.

The story finds its match in "The wolf and the Lamb" of the Aesop's Fables. A wolf and a lamb were drinking water of the same stream flowing down a mountain. The wolf stood at a much higher elevation of the stream than the lamb. Seeing the lamb, the wolf wanted to devour him. He accused the lamb of contaminating his drinking water. The lamb pointed out that he was at the lower level of the stream than the wolf and that the water flows down the stream only. Hence, there was no chance for him to contaminate the water in any way. The wolf then accused the lamb of abusing him a year ago. The lamb replied that his age being less than a year, it was not possible for him to abuse the wolf. The wolf then asserted that it must have been the lamb's mother, who had abused him and it was the turn for the lamb to pay back now for the evil deeds of his mother. Saying this, the wolf pounced on the poor lamb and devoured him.

We observe lot of similarities between the tales of the Jataka and the Aesop's Fables. We have also observed that both Buddha and Aesop were almost of the same age. These compositions took place a few centuries after the death of the respective authors and there could have been mix up of the stories of the two countries. Moreover, prior to composition of these, a cultural linkage was also established between India and Greece due to the invasion of Alexander. Hence it is most likely that a few stories of Jataka might have found place in the Aesop's Fables in modified forms.

4.3 Jataka and the Arabian Nights.

In the Arabian language, the name of this great composition is "***Alif Laila wah Laila***". This is one of the internationally accredited compositions of olden days. Although it was composed in the Arabian country, it mentions about various stories connected to India, Turkey, Iran, Syria, Greece and China. As per the legend, the author of the Arabian Nights was a Queen *(Begum)* of an Emperor *(Sultan)* of the Persian country. Two princes named *Sahriar* and *Sahjaman* were the rulers of two parts of the country. Both of them got frustrated with their unchaste wives and the women folk as a whole. To take revenge on the womanhood, they used to marry a new wife every evening and behead her the next morning. One day, *Saharzad*, the daughter of the Chief Minister (*Wizard)* volunteered to become the Begum of the Sultan. Accordingly, she was married off to the Sultan. She came to the palace with her sister *Duniazad. Saharzad* had the capability of mesmerising the Sultan by story-telling every night. As a result, the Sultan kept her alive for one thousand and one nights. Meanwhile, she gave birth to three Sons. Thereafter, the Sultan stopped wife slaughtering and lived happily with the Begum. He got his brother *Sahjaman* married to his sister-in-law *Duniazad.* We shall now be going through the similar stories of both the compilations the Arabian Nights and the Jataka.

4.3.1 Losaka Jataka (*Losaka Jātaka - 41)* Mitravinda Jataka *(Mittavinda Jātaka - 82)*

Once upon a time, a Buddhist Brother was living in a village and was maintained well by the landlord. One day, there reached another brother and was also well treated by the land-lord. This made the former brother jealous and he ill-treated the newcomer. As a result, the former brother had to take many rebirths and had to undergo tremendous misery. After many rebirths as *Yaksha* and Dog, he had reborn as a human being again. His name was Mitravindaka. Wherever he used to stay, his neighbours had to face the nature's wrath because of his association and they ultimately used to drive him out. One day, he boarded a ship as an employee of that ship. After seven days of smooth sailing, the ship became stand still in the mid-ocean. The sailors came to know that this was due to the association with Mitravindaka. They deserted him in the sea on a bamboo raft. He found divine maidens in crystal palaces in islands. He spent some time merrily with them. He was not satisfied and wanted to have more fun. He sailed further and came to the city of Ogress. There, in a field, he found a goat, who was actually an Ogress. He tried to catch her to make a meal. The goat kicked him so vigorously that he landed in Benares. There he found King's goats grazing in a field. He thought that he could get back to the crystal palaces in the sea, where the divine maidens dwelt. To get a similar kick, he held the leg of a goat. The goatherds ran in and seized him mistaking for a goat-thief. The goat-herds were taking him to the King for punishment. Bodhisattva found him on the way and freed him.

4.3.2 Mitravinda Jataka *(Mittavinada Jātaka - 104)* Mitravinda Jataka *(Mittavinada Jātaka - 369)* Chatu-dwara Jataka *(Catu-dvāra Jātaka - 439)*

The tales as per these Jatakas have slight variations to the tale narrated above. In these, Mitravindaka is depicted as the son of a merchant having immense wealth. After the death of his father, he ill-treated his mother, bought a ship and sailed on the same. The ship got stranded in the mid-sea after seven day of smooth sailing and Mitravindaka was deserted on a bamboo-raft as in the previous story. He sailed further and reached crystal palaces, where he spent pleasant days in the company of the divine maidens. Thereafter, he sailed further in the search for more pleasure. Ultimately, he reached the *Ussada* Hell. He found a person there holding a razor-wheel over his head and doing penance for his evil deeds. *Mitravindaka* mistook it for a lotus bloom and thought that he could become the king of this lovely kingdom once he could snatch it away from the person and held it over his own head. He did so. The man, on getting relieved ran away to freedom. The wheel got fixed on Mitravindaka's head. He then realized that the wheel was a razor-wheel, meant to punish the guilty. *Bodhisattva* happened to visit the Ussada hell, when he found Mitravindaka holding the razor-wheel. He explained to Mitravindaka, the reasons for his punishment.

As per the Arabian Nights, there dwelt an immensely rich merchant named Sindbad in the city of Baghdad during the reign of the great Caliph (emperor) Harun-Al-Rashid. Sindbad's father was a wealthy merchant and Sindbad was his only child. After the death of his father, Sindbad spent all the wealth in worldly pleasures. One day he realized that almost all the wealth was spent barring a minor balance. He sold all the remaining belongings, bought some merchandise and set forth on a commercial voyage abroad a ship. The ship sailed to various ports and Sindbad did good business. One day, the sailors found a small island in the sea. They went there in boats and started cooking and relaxing. That island was actually the back of a giant Whale. As soon as that moved, people fell in the sea. Some got drowned some reached back the ship and sped away. Sindbad found himself deserted in the mid-sea. He could hold on to a wooden log and was carried away to an island. The main income of the Sultan of this island used to come from selling crossbreed horses produced out of unions of Mares and Walrus (Sea-horses). Sindbad was welcomed by the Sultan and was employed as the Chief of the seaport. One day, the ship, in which he sailed from Baghdad, arrived in that port. Sindbad's merchandise was kept intact in his box in the ship. He returned to Baghdad in that ship after earning a fortune. From these, he purchased a good house and other amenities.

After a few months, Sindbad purchased a ship and sailed again with his merchandise. For about two months, he visited various ports and sold the merchandise at a very high profit. While returning, he came across a beautiful green island with a hill at the centre. Sindbad went to that island with his co-passengers in small boats. He went around the island, took fruits and water and slept. When he woke up, he could not find the ship and he was left alone in the island. In the evening, a huge Roc flew in to the island and sat on a big white egg to incubate the same. It could not notice Sindbad. He tied himself to one leg of the roc with his turban. Next morning, the roc flew and landed on a mountain. Sindbad set himself free. The valley was infested with big snakes and innumerable glittering diamonds were strewn everywhere. Sindbad collected many diamonds, purchased another ship and returned to Baghdad with huge wealth.

After rest for a while, Sindbad sailed again for the third time. This time, the ship anchored near a tribal infested island. The tribal took possession of the ship, threw every one in the sea and sailed away. Sindbad and others found a palace in the island, entered in the same, and slept there. They had to face a cannibal demon and a huge python. All the sailors died except Sindbad. Next day a ship picked him up. This was fortunately the one, which deserted him during the second voyage. Sindbad's merchandise of the second voyage was kept there intact in the boxes. Sindbad returned to Baghdad with all those wealth.

After a year, again Sindbad set forth for the fourth time. This time, the ship was caught in a storm and perished. Sindbad, with a few companions reached ashore. They were caught by cannibal tribal and eaten. Sindbad somehow escaped and reached another island. Sultan of that island treated him well. He found that the inhabitants of that island did not know the use of bridle and rein. He prepared one for the Sultan's horse, which made the Sultan very happy. As proposed by the Sultan, Sindbad married a girl there. After a few days, when the wife died, both Sindbad and his wife were put in a deep death-well as per the custom of that country. Sindbad somehow managed to get out of the well of the dead. While escaping, he collected huge quantity of ornaments from the corpses. He could locate a ship, which brought him back to his home at Baghdad.

After a few months, Sindbad again sailed for the fifth time. This time, he purchased a ship and filled it with valuable merchandise form Basra. They earned unexpectedly good profits form trades aboard. While returning, the ship anchored near an island. Excepting Sindbad and the captain of the ship, others went to the island. There were two eggs of Rocs in the island. The sailors broke the eggs and carried the meat of the under grown fowls. Sindbad and the captain could smell the imminent danger and started sailing immediately to get away from the island as early as possible. By the time, the Rocs flew in carrying huge stones. One stone fell on the ship and the ship broke into pieces. Sindbad was again thrown into the sea. Somehow, he reached an island. There dwelt an old man, who managed to ride on Sindbad's shoulder and used him as his slave. Using his intelligence, Sindbad could kill him. One day, a ship came there. Sindbad boarded that for returning to Baghdad. On the way he got Coconuts, Sandalwood, Spices and Pearls through trading and earned a good fortune before returning home.

After a few months, a few foreign merchants visited Sindbad's home and informed that they were going to Hindustan. Sindbad accompanied them. After a few days of sailing, the ship was attracted by a magnetic mountain and was crushed on it. The ship broke into fragments. Sindbad survived. He came across a transparent river, with the riverbed filled with precious stones and gems. He filled these in a few sacks, made a wooden raft and sailed on the same in the river. The raft was caught in the high current and moved along the river at a high speed. The inhabitants of that area rescued the raft. The name of that country was Saran. He was taken to the Emperor of that country. The Emperor welcomed him and arranged for his return to Basra. He also sent lot of presentation for the Caliph Harun al Rashid.

Sindbad got tired of voyages and decided not to venture overseas any further. But, at the request of the Caliph, he had to set out again for the Saran Island with the return presentation form Harun al Rashid. He reached there without any problem. On the way back, the ship was invaded by pirates, who took all the valuables and made the voyagers slave. Sindbad was sold to a rich merchant. Sindbad helped the merchant a lot in hunting and made him very rich by giving him information about a massive stock of ivory. The merchant, in return, presented Sindbad half of the wealth. With this, Sindbad returned to Baghdad.

Thus, we find some similarities between the stories of

Mitravindaka in the Jataka and the stories of Sindbad of the Arabian Nights. Some scholars feel that the Mitravindaka of the Jātakas has become Sindbad in the Arabian Nights.

4.3.3 Benuka Jataka *(Veḷuka Jātaka - 43)*

Once upon a time, Bodhisattva used to live in a hermitage in the Himalayan region as an ascetic with five hundred followers. One day, a young poisonous snake came wondering to the hut of a brother, who started rearing it in a bamboo cage as his own son. When Bodhisattva came to know about it, he warned the brother of the imminent danger and asked him to refrain from continuing with this. The brother was not convinced and he continued to rear the serpentine. One day, the brother, along with others had gone to the forest to fetch some fruits. The snake became angry due to hunger. When the brother returned, he went to fondle and feed the snake. The snake bit his foster father to death and escaped in the jungle.

As in the Arabian Nights, a pedestrian found a poisonous snake lying on a roadside in a precarious condition for want of food for a long period. The pedestrian felt pity on the snake and he brought it to his home. He nursed the snake well and made it healthy in two days by feeding him good food. When the snake regained its vitality, it attacked its saviour and bit him to death.

4.3.4 Radha Jataka *(Rādha Jātaka - 145)*

Once Bodhisattva took birth as a parrot and was named Posthapada. He, along with his brother Radha, dwelt in a Brahmin's house. They were being treated by the Brahmin as his own sons. Once, the Brahmin went out of town on a business for a few days. During his absence, his unchaste wife kept on merry making with the outsiders. When the Brahmin returned, Posthapada narrated him the entire story and flew away with his brother.

4.3.5 Radha Jataka *(Rādha Jātaka - 198)*

In this story, Bodhisattva had born as a parrot named Radha. His brother was Posthapada. They resided in a Brahmin's house. When the Brahmin went out for a few days, his unchaste wife got engaged in immoral activities with the outsiders. Seeing this, Posthapada advised her to refrain from such activities. The wife got angry and in the guise of fondling him, killed Posthapada by twisting his neck. She then threw the dead bird in the oven to destroy evidences. When the Brahmin returned, Radha apprised him of the entire incident and flew away.

As in the Arabian Nights, a merchant had an extremely beautiful wife. One day he bought a parrot from the market, who could narrate in human language whatever he witnessed. The merchant kept the parrot in his wife's room and set out on a business tour. As soon as the merchant had gone away the wife called her paramour and had unlimited fun with him. When the merchant returned, the bird narrated the love story of his wife. The merchant beat his wife for her misdeeds and again set out on business for a night. The wife covered the bird's cage with a black cloth. She also ordered a maid to keep on rotating the grinding stone throughout the night and asked another maid to keep on pouring water form one pot to the other. The sounds resembled rain and thunderstorm. When the Merchant returned, the Parrot said that there were heavy rain and storm throughout the last night. The Merchant knew that there were neither any rain nor any thunderstorm in the previous night and concluded that the parrot was a liar. He felt sorry for beating his wife believing the parrot. He killed the parrot and apologized to his wife. Later on, he came to know the character of his wife and repented for killing parrot.

4.3.6 Kuta-banijya Jataka *(Kūta-vāṇija Jātaka - 218)*

Once upon a time, two traders, one from a village and the other from a town were friends. One day, the trader from the village came to his friend in the town and kept five hundred ploughshares with him. When the friend went away, the townsman sold these and kept the money with him. He then sprinkled some mouse-dung in the storage yard. When the villager returned and asked for the ploughshares, he showed him the place filled with the mouse-dung and said that the mice had eaten the ploughshares. The villager understood the background story but did not show any dissidence. He took the son of the townsman with him and said that he was going to the river bank for a bath. But instead of going to the river, he went to another friend's house and kept his friend's son there. He then returned to the townsman and reported that a hawk had carried away his son from the riverbank. The townsman could not believe this story and took his friend to the Court of Justice. The Judge asked as to how a hawk could carry away a grown up boy? The villager replied that if the mice could eat the ploughshares, why not a hawk could carry away his friend's son. On enquiry by the Judge, he narrated the story. The Judge ordered the townsman to return the ploughshares and villager the boy. They did accordingly and the case got settled.

As in the Arabian Nights, a merchant sold all his properties and got ten thousand Guineas (gold coins). He poured those gold coins in a pitcher and kept it in a friend's storeroom. He poured some green Olives on the upper layers of the pitcher and closed the lid. He went to Mecca and other countries and returned after seven years. Meanwhile, one day, the friend's Wife longed to have some olives. The husband went to the market but could not get the same. He then remembered of the olives kept by his friend in the pitcher. When he opened the lid he found that all the olives had got rotten. He discovered the gold coins underneath the rotten olives. He took out all the gold coins, bought green olives, filled the pitcher with those and closed the lid. When the Merchant returned, he found that the gold coins had vanished and only the green olives remained there. The Merchant went to the court of a *Qazi*, who ruled that the friend was not guilty since there was no evidence that the gold coins were really kept in the pitcher. The Merchant approached the Caliph (emperor) for justice. The Caliph, while out an evening walk, found a few children acting as the *Qazi* and the two merchants were performing mock trial of the case. The Caliph was astonished to observe that the child acting as *Qazi* had the wisdom to identify the culprit. Next morning, the child was called in the Caliph's court to conduct the trial. The boy asked the merchant's friend to produce before the court the pitcher containing the olives. The friend did so. The boy then asked an olive-trader to tell the probable age of the Olives. The Traders vouched that the Olives were fresh and could not be seven years old. The Merchant's friend accepted to the guilt and returned the gold coins.

4.3.7 Kharaputra Jataka *(Kharaputta Jātaka - 386)*

Once upon a time, a king named Senaka reigned in Benares. He got a charm form the Serpent-king that he would be able to understand the languages of all types of living beings. The Serpent-king also cautioned that, in case the king divulged the charm to anyone else, he would die by fire. Thereafter, the king was able to understand the language of all types of creatures including the ants. One day, the king was taking cake, molasses and honey in the breakfast. A drop each of molasses and honey and a small particle of cake fell on the floor. An ant, finding these, cried out in joy, "The king's cake cart has broken, also broken are molasses cart and honey jars". The ant's kinsmen came out of their hideouts in a procession to carry away these to their abode. Hearing this, the king laughed. Later, a fly invited his wife to have love. She replied that, the king's feet would be powdered. They would put the fragrance on their body from the floor and then make love sitting on the king's back. This made the king to laugh to his heart's content. Again, while having lunch, a small lump of rice fell on the ground. Seeing this, an ant cried, "Come quickly, the king's rice wagon has broken". These made the king to laugh again and again. When he laughed, the queen was with him. She got curious and wanted to know the reasons for laughing. When the king disclosed that he knew the charm to understand the languages of all living beings, the queen pestered him to tell it to her. The king said that if he divulged the charm to anyone else, he would die. The queen replied that she was interested to learn the charm and she hardly bothered whether the king survived or died. The king then decided to teach it to the queen and die. Hearing this, the god king Indra descended on the earth with his wife as a goat couple. When the king went out in his chariot, the goat couple came on the way of the chariot and pretended to have sex. The chariot's horse scolded the goats saying they were fools and did not have the sense as to where to have sex. The he goat retorted that the horse was a greater fool because he carried the chariot as a slave. The goat also said that the king was the greatest fool as he was preparing to sacrifice his life for the queen. Once the king died, neither the king nor the queen would achieve anything. The goat instead advised the king to lashing his wife for such irresponsible demand. The king understood all conversations. He went back to the palace. He asked the queen to get prepared to receive the charm. As a precondition she would be given one hundred lashings. The king ordered the servants to start lashing the queen. After enduring two or three strokes, the queen said that she no longer wanted to have the charm. The king did not listen. He ordered lashing the queen till the skin at her back was peeled off.

As in the 'Arabian Nights', a farmer knew the languages of the animals. One day he overheard the conversation between his bullock and the donkey. The bullock said that unlike the donkey he had to toil hard all day long in the field, whereas, the donkey was much luckier with very little work. The donkey advised the bullock that while going to the field the bullock should feign illness so that he could be excused from hard work. The farmer laughed. Next day, while taking the bullock to the field, he pretended to be ill as planned. The farmer kept him back in the cowshed and took the donkey to the field to perform the job of the bullock. The inexperienced donkey's condition became very bad. After two days of hard working, he told the bull that the farmer had decided to sell the bull to a butcher, since he had lost the capability to work. Hearing this, the bull went to the work the next day as usual. The farmer also heard this and laughed. His wife asked him the reason for laughing. The farmer said that he would die if he divulged the truth. His wife insisted on hearing the reason and said that she was hardly bothered if he survived or died. The farmer prepared to die and met all his kith and kin. He overheard the conversation between his dog and the cock. The dog was scolding the cock for having fun with his fifty hens even if the owner prepared to die. The cock said that he had the power to tackle his fifty wives. If any of the hens misbehaved even slightly, he pecked her with his beaks, so that they behaved properly. On the other hand, the farmer was unable to control even one wife. I would have bashed my wife black and blue, if I were the farmer, the hen asserted. Hearing this, the farmer went back house with a stick and beat his wife black and blue for her illogical demand. The wife gave up the demand and never harboured such illogical wishes thereafter.

4.3.8 Samudra Jataka *(Sàmugga Jātaka - 436)*

Once upon a time, Bodhisattva had been leading the life of an ascetic. He was living in a hermitage in the Himalayas. A demon lived nearby. He used to kill the people and eat them. He, however, used to visit Bodhisattva to listen to his preaching of laws. One day, a beautiful lady was passing by that area with a group of bodyguards. Seeing the demon approaching, the men threw their weapons and ran away to safety. Finding the beautiful lady alone, the demon took her to his abode and married her. The demon used to keep her in a big basket, which he swallowed and preserved in his belly. One day he went to a lake, eructed out the basket from his stomach and took out the lady. He bathed the lady and anointed her body with perfumes. He left her outside the basket and went to lake for bathing. At that time, Wind's son, who was a magician was overflying her with his magical sword. Seeing him, the lady enticed him and kept him in the basket. When the demon returned, she got into the basket as usual and laid herself over the magician's body. The demon was unaware of the presence of the magician. He swallowed the basket as usual, and proceeded for his abode. On the way he stopped at Bodhisattva's hermitage for a while. Bodhisattva, through his supernatural powers, could see the presence of the magician inside the demon's belly, who was having a good time with the lady. Being told by Bodhisattva about this, the demon eructed out the basket and found the magician inside it. Being scared of the powers of the magicians, he let the magician off. Being disgusted with the character of the lady, he also deserted her.

As in the Arabian Nights, Sultan Sahjaman and his brother Sahriar got disgusted with their unchaste wives, left the kingdom and reached seashore. While relaxing under a tree, they found a huge demon coming out of the sea with a big box on his head. The scared brothers took shelter on a tree branch. The demon sat under the tree and unlocked the box. A beautiful lady came out of the box. The tired demon kept his head on the lap of the lady and slept. He started snoring almost instantaneously. The lady, finding the two brothers, signalled them to come down. She then ordered both the brothers to have sex with her. When they refused, the lady threatened to kill them by awakening the demon. Hence, both the brothers had to obey and satisfy her. Upon enjoying sex delightfully, she collected the rings of these two new lovers, which added on to her existing collection of 570 rings from the earlier lovers.

MAHA-UMMAGA JATAKA

5.0 JATAKA IN THE RETROSPECT

5.1 Insight form the Jataka

5.1.1 Places of Narration

Out of 547 numbers of Jatakas, most of the stories (441 Nos.) were narrated by the blessed one at the Jetavana, followed by Venuvana (46 Nos.). The balance 60 numbers Jatakas were told in as many as 35 other places.

5.1.2 Forms of former births

We come across a total of 562 births by Bodhisattva in the 547 stories. The statistics points out that, Bodhisattva had born as God / Buddha / Dharma / god Indra and other human beings of respectable status 385 times. Balance 177 times he took births as human beings of interior-strata, such as; thief, animals, birds, serpent, aquatic creatures etc. There are total 87 forms of birth as enlisted in the respective section.

It is worth mentioning that, all the Jataka stories were written after the Mahaparinirbana of the Lord. In the Jatakas listed initially, Bodhisattva had born only as a respectable person and not as an animal or person of lower strata. The list of the Jataka stories gradually swelled, which included all such inferior characters also.

5.1.3 Multiplicity of births

In the Chitta-Sambhuta Jataka (No. 498), we observe that Bodhisattva took birth four times in different roles. They are; cremator (Chandala) stag, osprey and ascetic. We also observed that Bodhisattva took birth twice in twelve Jataka stories.

5.1.4 Places referred to

It is observed that, out of the 547 Nos. Jatakas, in 543

Nos., some place of occurrence of incidence have been referred to. The names of such places have been enlisted. Benares seems to have been the most favoured place appearing in 441 numbers Jatakas, followed by Mithila - 19 times and Rajagriha - 11 times. Other 48 places have single digit scores.

It is also observed that Benares was called in seven other names, i,e; Molini, Surundha-nagara, Ramma-nagara, the village of Carpenters (Suttadhara-gāma), Sudarsana-nagara, Brahmabardhana and Puspavati (Pupphavatī).

5.1.5 Reigning Kings

Most of the Jatakas mention the names of the kings reigning at the time of the occurrence of the story. Total 52 kings' names are mentioned in 495 Jatakas. King Brahmadatta finds place in 399 numbers Jatakas, followed by Vedeharaj (14). Other 50 kings have single digit scores.

Many kings of the Ramayana, the Mahabharata and other pre-Buddha literature also found place in the list.

5.1.6 Repetition of Titles

As enlisted in the respective section, the titles of many Jataka stories are repeated. From the count, it is found that 38 titles are repeated in 93 Jatakas.

5.1.7 Stories Revisited

Similarities between the Jātaka tales have already been enlisted. Total No. of the Jatákas involved in such similarities is 216. These 216 number Jatakas originate form 87 stories. Hence, if we eliminate the repetitions, we get 547 - (216-87) = 418 stories, which are non-repetitive.

5.1.8 Important Occasions

The blessed one had narrated the Jataka tales, whenever situations warranted. In fact, every occasion was important enough for the Lord to bless the mankind with his preaching in the form of a Jataka story. However, some extremely important occasions are identified, when such a necessity arose. These occasions include; show of supernatural power by the Buddha, to dissuade two rival groups from war, solving complex problems faced by various kings, Devadatta's punishment by the god, stretching on the death bed, meeting king Suddhadhona and wife Yashodhara after attaining Buddha-hood etc. 25 such occasions have been identified and discussed.

5.2 Jataka's Relationship with Ancient Indian Literature

5.2.1 Relationship with the Ramayana

Although there are traces of the Ramayana in various Jatakas, we have selected a few with significant resemblances.

Devadharma Jataka (6) and the Dasaratha Jataka (461) resemble Rama's going to exile at the wish of the step-mother and becoming king later. Jayaddisa Jataka (513) and Sarabhanga Jataka (522) resounds the Dandaka episode of the Ramayana. Alambusa Jataka (523) and Nalinika Jataka narrate the tale of Rishwashringa Muni of the Ramayana. Sama Jataka (540) is the depiction of killing of Andhaka Muni's son by Dasaratha etc.

5.2.2 Relationship with the Mahabharata

Relationship between the Jataka and the Mahabharata is even more than that with the Ramayana. As many as twenty Jatakas share close relationships, while eight others use the names of persons, places of the Mahabharata.

We recapitulate the relationships between the two as already studied.

A part of the Devadharma Jataka (6) corroborates with Dharma's asking question to Yudhisthira in the Mahabharata. Kasthahari Jataka (7) is the story of Dusmanta and Shakuntala. Mitachinti Jataka (114) is the replica of the story of the "Three Fishes". Bilara Jataka (128) and Agnika Jataka (129) closely resemble the story of Dindika, the Cat. Rajovada Jataka (151) is similar to the story of the kings Suhotra and Sibi. Silamimansa Jataka (330) relates to the Mahabharata's story of a hawk's leaving a piece of meat and of the maid named Pingala. Kuntani Jataka (343) is similar to the story of the Pujani bird. Sutanu Jataka (398) is traced in the Mahabharata's story of the killing of the Vaka demon by Bhima. Mahasuka Jataka (429) and Chullasuka Jataka (430) find their origin in the story of "The Parrot" in the Mahabharata. Krishna-dwipayana Jataka (444) has originated from the story of Mandavya Muni. Ghata Jataka (454) is the story of Yaduvamsa, Kamsa, the life of Krishna and the ruin of the Yaduvamsa. Bhisa Jataka (488) is a shadow of the story of "Stealing of Lotus-Stalk" of the Mahabharata. Sivi Jataka (499) is the story of the King Sivi of the Mahabharata. Alambusa Jataka (523) and Nalinika Jataka (526) depict the story of Rishwashringa Muni. In the Kundala Jataka (536), Draupadi has been portrayed as a woman of bad character. Mahasutasoma Jataka (537) is the story of the king Kalmaspada of the Mahabharata, who turned into a man-eater.

Thus there are many resemblances with stories of the Mahabharata.

5.2.3 Relationship with the Bhagabata

The Bhagabata and the Mahabharata share many stories and incidents in a coherent manner. The Bhagabata encompasses the life stories of Lord Vishnu during his various Avataras on the earth. A portion of the story of the Avataras, i.e. as 'Krishna' is depicted in the Mahabharata. Hence, only those resemblances with the Bhagabata, which have not featured in the study of the Mahabharata, have featured in this chapter.

Mrigapotaka Jataka (372) finds its origin in the story of King Bharata, who, after renouncing the world grew affection on an orphaned fawn. Ghata Jataka (454) is the depiction of the life history of Lord Krishna. It narrates the dynasty of Kamsa, birth of Krishna, killing of Kamsa by Krishna, formation and growth of Yadu kingdom at

Dwaravati, the ruin of Yaduvamsa, death of Balarama and Krishna etc. Some changes have been incorporated in the story of Bhagavata. Devaki has been renamed as Devagarbha, Nanda's wife Yasoda has become Nandagopa etc. Stories have also got changed as per the need. The theme of Nimi Jataka (541) matches with the story of King Nimi in the Bhagavata. The description of the hell and various punishments meted out for various offences corroborate with the version of the Bhagavata.

These Jatakas find their root in the Bhagavata.

5.2.4 Relationship with the Panchatantra

The Panchatantra is a post-Buddha compilation. Nine of its stories match with the Jatakas. One of the stories matches both with the Jataka as well as with the Mahabharata.

The story of "The Stork and the Crab" of the Panchatantra corroborates with the "Baka Jataka (38)". The story of the "Three Fish" is more similar to the Mahabharata's "Anagata Bidhata" than the "Mitachinti Jataka (114)". The story of "The Lion Makers" resembles the Sanjiva Jataka (206)". "The Tortoise and the Geese" is a replica of the "Kacchapa-Jataka (215)". "The Mice that ate Iron" has hardly any difference with the "Kuta-Vanijya Jataka (218)". "The Monkey and the Crocodile" in based on "Vanarinda Jataka (57)", "Sumsumara Jataka (208)" and "Vanara Jataka (342)". "The cave that Talked" is similar to the second part of the "Vanarinda Jataka".

Excepting the story of the "Three Fish", all others mentioned above have been sourced from the Jataka.

5.2.5 Relationship with the Hitopadesa

The Hitopadesa was composed after the Panchatantra

and have many stories identical to it. Five stories of the Hitopadesa have been identified for their similarities with the Jataka.

"The story of a Crow, a Deer and a Jackal" is similar to the "Triparyastha Mriga Jataka (16)". "The story of a Hunter, a Crow, some Doves and a Mouse" is a replica of the "Sammodamana Jataka (33)". "The story of a Washer-man and an unlucky Donkey" is a slightly changed version of the Sinha-Charma Jataka (189)". The story of "Birds and the shivering Monkeys" finds its origin in the Kutidushaka Jataka (321). The story of the "Sandhibheda Jataka (349)" is found in the refined form in the "Suhridbheda" chapter of the Hitopadesa in the name of "The story of a rich Merchant, his Bull, a Lion and a Jackal". Hence, the above stories of the Hitopadesa and a few more already enlisted under the Panchatantra owe their origin to the Jataka.

5.2.6 Relationship with the Kathasaritsagara

Kathasaritsagara is composed after the Hitopadesa and mentions about Jataka stories. It contains thirteen stories similar to the Jataka. These are Chullaka-Sresthi Jataka (4), Sammodamana Jataka (33), Baka Jataka (38), Mitachinti Jataka (114), Sinha-Charma Jataka (189), Kuranga Mriga Jataka (206), Sishumara Jataka (208), Vanara Jataka (342), Kachhapa Jataka (215), Kuta Vanijya Jataka (218), Uluka Jataka (270), Sandhibheda Jataka (349) and Unmadayanti Jataka (527). It has been observed that all the stories excepting the Mitachinti Jataka (114) have been originated from the Jataka and some of these have reached the Kathasaritsagara via the Panchatantra and the Hitopadesa.

5.3 Jataka's Relationship with Ancient Foreign Literature

5.3.1 Relationship with the Odyssey

Odyssey was composed much before the birth of Buddha. There is no significant resemblance of any part of a story with that of the Jataka. A few remote coincidences do not conclusively testify any relationship between the two.

5.3.2 Aesop's Fables

Although Aesop and Buddha were contemporary, Aesop's Fables were compiled much later in the Alexandria Library by the scholars. While compiling these, any fable available through oral communication might have made inroads in the compilation of Aesop's Fables. It may be noted that post invasion of Alexander in India, there had been export of some amount of literature among others. Aesop's Fables bear similarities with sixteen Jatakas, namely; Munika Jataka (30), Saluka Jataka (128), Agnika Jataka (129), Suvarnahamsa Jataka (136), Virochana Jataka (143), Jambuka Jataka (335), Sinha-Charma Jataka (189), Kachhapa Jataka (215), Jambu-Khadaka Jataka (294), Anta Jataka (295), Javasakuna Jataka (308), Kukkuta Jataka (383), Dhumkari Jataka (413) and Dipi Jataka (426). It is quite obvious that, the Jataka stories had infiltrated in large scale in the Aesop's Fables compilation.

5.3.3 The Arabian Nights

"The Arabian Nights" was composed around 900 - 1000 AD. As many as eleven stories have distinct similarities with the Jataka. These are; Losaka Jataka (41), Mitravinda

Jataka (82, 104, 369), Chatu-dwara Jataka (439), Venuka Jataka (43), Radha Jataka (145 & 198), Kuta-Vanijya Jataka (218), Kharaputra Jataka (386) and Samudra Jataka (436). It is quite obvious that these Jataka stories have made their place in this compilation also.

5.4 Summary

- From the selected comparative studies we observe that the Blessed One had chosen stories from those existed during his time, refined and reproduced them after incorporating necessary changes to suit the requirements of preaching the Noble path. It is quite obvious that the Noble Soul wanted to show the Right Path to the mankind rather than telling stories from the point of view as a literature maker. Hence, we find that the portions of the stories have been sourced from the Ramayana, the Mahabharata and the Bhagabata.

- It is known to us that Gautama Buddha's Sakya clan had originated from the Ikshaku Dynasty, which was Hindu by religion. Later on, the Lord Buddha proposed Buddhism, which incorporated good teachings and eliminated evil parts of the Hinduism like Caste-ism, sacrifice of animals in the name of religion etc. Prince Gautama had grown up in the existing Hindu environment and thoroughly studied all the mythological compositions. He had profound knowledge in all the existing literatures of his time and knew as many as sixty-four scripts. He was sent to the most renowned and knowledgeable teacher named Viswamitra for education.

- The above facts corroborate that the stories and fables existed at the time of composition of the Jataka were widely used in it. Subsequently, many legendary compositions in India and abroad like the Panchatantra, the Hitopadesa, the Kathasaritsagara, the Aesop's Fables and the Arabian Nights etc. also used some of the Jataka stories in the compositions.

- The selected studies Vis-á-vis foreign literature does not prove their influence on the Jataka. Rather, the foreign literature such as; the Aesop's Fables, the Arabian Nights etc. adapted Jataka stories. Thus the stories of Mitravindaka in the Jataka fail to establish links with the voyage of Odysseus in Odyssey, but Sindbad's stories in the Arabian Nights reveal close ties with the Jatakas. The Aesop's Fables owe a lot to the Jataka with many stories being copied without significant deviations.

5.5 Jataka in the Retrospect

- We have noticed that the Jataka is not an original compilation of short or long stories for the purpose of story telling or for sheer creation of literature. On the other hand, the existing stories along with the new ones have been used by the Great Soul exclusively to impart the lessons of true values of life, e.g. Charity (*Dāna*) Morality (*Sila*), Salutation (*Nekkhamma*), Wisdom (*Paññā*), Exertion (*Virya*), Forgiveness (*Ksānti*), Amity (*Mettā*), Truth (*Sacca*), Resolution (*Adhisthāna*) and Equanimity (*Upekkhā*).
- The blessed one worked relentlessly to convert the world to a better and peaceful place to live in with amity, love and mutual respect. He used the Jataka stories as vehicles for propagation of the ideal lessons. For this purpose, he did not hesitate to change and modify the stories. We also observe that the Lord has told the same stories more than once after changing the subject matter substantially. This is due to the fact that, each story was tailor-made to give a particular message in a particular situation. We observe with great astonishment that Tathagata resolved even the most complex and critical problems in the most simple and unambiguous manner. He used the common man's language in the most simple and lucid yet most interesting way. With the help of these stories, he could achieve many objectives, like; changing the minds of the heinous people like Ajatasatru - who tortured and killed his own father, refrained the kings from animal sacrifice, bringing amity between two warring groups, bringing peace and tranquillity in the minds of the bereaved family members, who have lost their nearest and dearest ones, etc. The list is very large. In fact,

there is a solution in the Jataka for almost all types of problems; those could be faced by the mankind or other environmental beings. Through the Jataka, Tathagata had advised the human beings to be friendly with the animals, birds, other beings and the nature as a whole. He objected to indiscriminate mining, cutting of trees, killing of animals, unkind behaviour to other etc. He has tried to persuade the people to be on the right path by depicting the terrible punishments meted out in the hell for evil deeds. He has also depicted the luxurious living in the heaven for the people following the righteous path.

★ The Jataka is also unique in its style. Usage of the most simplistic Pali language has brought it nearer to the heart of the masses. Its simple, lucid and free-flowing expression makes the reader visualize the events as if being presented on a TV screen. Addition of appropriate verses (*Gāthās*) in between have also evoked greater interest in the minds of the readers and added to the literary values.

★ The presentation of the Jataka is simply unparallel. Each Jataka story is divided into three sections. '*Pachupanna-vatthu*' or the present circumstance, which led Tathagata to narrate the story, has historic value. It not only depicts the historic background but also evokes keen quest for the '*Atitavatthu*' or the story itself. '*Samodhāna*' or casting the present characters into the roles of the previous birth stories drags the suspense till the end.

★ Listening to the Jatakas benefited the audience instantaneously. Each story was powered enough to transform the target listener and could advance others a few steps in their path of salvation. Many a times a sure disaster could be averted by telling a Jataka story. The characteristics discussed above have put the Jataka on the topmost slot in its class.

* It is worth noting that the characters like Devadatta, who wanted to strangulate the process of peace and amity by killing the ambassador of peace and the benefactor of the people of the world, have born time and again in various forms and had tried to kill the Avataras like Rama, Krishna, Jesus, Mohammed etc. They are even scared of the shadows of peace and amity and try to wipe them out of the world. Added to these, the huge stockpiles of devastating atomic weaponry threaten the existence of the very mankind today.
* The Jataka was not only relevant in the past; it is highly relevant in the today's world as well. It is not meant for any particular Caste, Creed, Religion, Language or Geographic area. Its study is highly beneficial to any person irrespective of his social, political, financial or religions status. We do hope that the entire world shall derive immense benefit from the teachings of the greatest teacher of all times.

6.0 GLOSSARY

Agnika : A tuft of hair left on the clean shaven head (usually sported by Hindu Priests).

Ajatasatru : He was the son of king Bimbisara. He tortured and killed his father to ascend to the throne on the advice of Devadatta.

Altar : Chopping block

Anathapindika : The Sanskrit name is Anathapindada. He hailed from a business family from Sravasti. His original name was Sudatta. Once, he chanced to meet Buddha at the Winter Cottage at Rajagriha. He was so moved by seeing Buddha; he became his ardent follower immediately. He constructed Jetavana Vihara, a beautiful monastery for the Buddhist Sangha at a huge cost.

Most of the Jataka stories have been told in this monastery.

Asvamedha Yagna : This ritual used to be performed by an emperor who considered himself invincible. The army used to travel through various kingdoms with a hybrid horse (Asva) representing the emperor. The kingdoms, which allowed the horse to pass through, were deemed to have surrendered to the emperor. Any one obstructing the horse deemed to challenge the emperor and had to fight with his army. Upon successful return of the horse, a yagna or puja used to be performed by sacrificing the holy horse and the emperor was declared as invincible.

Badrikarama : This monastery was situated in the city of *Kosambi* located on the bank of the river *Yamuna* at 35 miles North-West of Allahabad.

Bharata : Bharata was son of king Dushyanta and Shakuntala, who was a great king of India long ago.

Bhikkhu : is a Buddhist monk, who lives in a monastery and earns his livelihood by begging (*Bhiksha).*

Bimbisara : He was the king of Magadha. He ascended to the throne at the age of 16. He became a disciple of Buddha at the age of 29. He was six years younger than Buddha. Bimbisara gifted Venuvana to Buddhist Sangha. He loved his son Ajatasatru very much. But at the advice of Devadatta, Ajatasatru imprisoned his father and forced him to die by starvation at the age of 65.

Bisakha : She was the daughter of a very rich businessman named Dhananjay, who used to live in the Anga country. Buddha visited Anga and delivered his discourse. Bisakha was 7 years old at that time. She became an ardent follower of Buddha on hearing the discourse. She was married off to Purnabardhan, son of a businessman named Mrigar, who resided at Sravasti. Bisakha sold all the ornaments, she brought from her parental home as wedding gift. She constructed a Buddhist monastery named Purbarama (Eastern Park) on the eastern fringe of Sravasti and dedicated the same to Buddha. She had enormous physical and mental strength and could control even a rampaging elephant by holding its trunk. She gave birth to ten sons and ten daughters.

Bodhisattva : *Gautama Buddha* had to take births several hundred times between his vouching to become "*Buddha*" and the actual enlightenment under the *Bodhi* tree near *Urubilva* village. He had to descend on the earth again and again to practise the ten "*Paramitas*". The forms in which he had to be reborn include; Animals, Birds, Trees, Serpents, Aquatic creatures, Human beings of inferior strata, Businessmen, Gentlemen, Kings, Gods etc. During these births, the Buddha is known as "*Bodhisattva*" or "*Buddhankura*". In every birth he did something good for the mankind, society or nature. Thereby he got himself elevated to a better birth next time. This had gradually advanced him towards fulfilment of the ten *Paramitas.* His last birth on this earth was as *Gautama Buddha*, after which he attained '*Nirvana*' or freedom from rebirths on the earth.

Boisterous : Turbulent (weather).

Buddha : As per Buddhist philosophy, Buddhas descend on the earth at various time spans ranging innumerable years. One has to take birth in various forms of living beings and practice 10 Paramitas (code of conduct) to take birth as a Buddha. Gautama Buddha was the last Buddha. The next Buddha shall appear after many more years.

Calypso : As per Greek mythology, she was a beautiful nymph. She used to reside in the Ogygia Island. After the Trojan War, when Odysseus was returning home, he happened to reach Ogygia. He had to spend long seven years in the company of Calypso, who wanted to have him as his immortal husband. But on pressurisation by Gods, she had to release him. She also made arrangement for a boat, food and beverages for Odysseus for his return journey to home.

Circe : As per Greek mythology, she is a demi goddess. She is the goddess of magic and daughter of Sun god Helios. Circe is well known for magic wand/herbs. She could transform her enemies into animals.

Cyclops : As per Greek/Roman mythology a Cyclops is a one-eyed primitive demon, which has only one eye in his forehead. The literal meaning is 'Circle-eyed'. In Odyssey, the hero Odysseus encountered such a creature and was able to get out of his clutch.

Dasharatha : He is a character in the Ramayana. He was the king of Ayodhya and the father of Rama. He had four sons from his three queens. As per the wish of his second queen, he had to send his eldest son Rama to forest for fourteen years and the younger prince Bharata became the king. When Rama went to the forest, Dasharatha's heart broke and he breathed his last.

Devadatta : He was Buddha's brother in law. He embraced Buddhism after 2 or 3 years of Gautama's attaining Buddha-hood. He became the arch rival of Buddha. He made friendship with king Bimbisara's son Ajatasatru. At his provocation, Ajatasatru imprisoned his own father and became the king. Ajatasatru forced his father to die out of starvation. Devadatta attempted to kill Buddha thrice by sending archers, letting loose a drunk elephant named Nalagiri upon him and finally releasing a huge block of stone from the cliff of a hill on Buddha. All his attempts to kill Buddha failed. Ultimately, Devadatta went to meet Buddha and seek his pardon. But as soon as he landed in front of Buddha's monastery, the earth split where he stood and a huge flame engulfed Devadatta and took him to the hell.

Dhananjay : Dhananjay is the other name of Arjun, the third Pandava, who was a great archer and a famous warrior character in the Mahabharata.

Drudgery : Slavery or very mean laborious work.

Dwaravati : Dwaravati was the kingdom of Sri Krishna. The place is located in Gujarat and it is now known as Dwarka.

Eraka plant : It is a light weight straw type plant, which grows in marshy land.

Fowler : A fowler is professional hunter, who catches, hunts or kills fowls.

Gandharbha marriage : In case, a male and a female love each other and get married through premarital sex is called Gandharbha Marriage.

Ghositarama or Ghosita Park : It was adjacent to the ancient city of *Kosambi*, situated at 30 miles Northwest of Allahabad. King *Udayan* used to reign in *Kosambi.* His minister *Ghosita* (or *Ghosil*) presented this adjoining garden to the Buddhist *Sangha.* This was known as *Ghositarama* or *Ghosita* Park. King Udayan got a Buddha statue curved out of red sandalwood during the lifetime of the Lord.

Goblin : A sprite or a demon.

Goshringi : Goshringi was a disciple of Buddha. He donated a massive garden of Saal trees to Buddha. The garden was known as Mahavan and was situated near Vesali. A monastery named Kutagarsala was built there. Buddha used to stay there at times.

Grijjhakuta Parbata : This place is also known as the Vulture peak. This was situated on the outskirts of *Rajagriha* (modern Rajgir) in *Magadha* kingdom in the state of Bihar. *Devadatta* tried to kill the Blessed One here in connivance with King *Ajatasatru*, who killed his father *Bimbisara.*

Hall of Hades : As per the Greek mythology, Hall of Hades is the place where all the departed souls lived. Odysseus visited this place and got lot of information from them.

Hamlet : A small settlement of people, not big enough to be called a village.

Jetavana : *Jetavana* was a garden situated near the town of *Sravasti.* It was transformed into a *"Mahavihara"* or a great monastery for Buddha.

It was a square shaped garden measuring one thousand

hands in length on each side. It contained a *Gandhakuti* (Perfumed chamber) at the centre, which was the abode of Lord Buddha. It was surrounded by eighty (80) dwelling places for *Mahatheras*, Guest houses, Prayer halls, Hostels for *Bhikkhus*, Walkways, Ponds and other necessary facilities for living.

It was built and donated by a rich man named *Anatha-Pindika*. He became a disciple of the Master at *Rajagriha* and humbly requested him to be his guest at *Sravasti*.

After returning to *Sravasti*, *Anatha-Pindika* wanted to buy this garden from the owner named *Jetu Kumara*. In exchange, *Jetu Kumara* demanded gold coins enough to cover the whole land, which was complied by *Anatha-Pindika* at a cost of 18 Crores (1 Crore = 10 millions) of such coins. He spent another 18 Crores of gold coins to build the complex. The distance between *Rajagriha* and *Jetavana* was 45 yojanas (1 yojana = 7 miles). *Anatha-Pindika* built rest houses at every yojana at the cost of one lakh gold coins each, so that *Tathagata* could take rest conveniently during his journey between the two places. *Anatha-Pindika* also arranged a grand inauguration ceremony of this monastery when he dedicated this to the Buddhist Sangha.

It is said that *Jetu Kumara* became repentant later for charging unreasonable price for this land. He built four seven storied palaces at the four corners of *Jetavana* for Buddha with the price he got. Lord spent most of his time in this monastery.

Jivaka : Abhay had born out of union of king Bimbisara and a prostitute. Jivaka had born out of union between Abhay and a prostitute named Salavati. After the birth of Jivaka, Salavati deserted him in a jungle. He was found by

Abhay in the midst of crows. Abhay reared up the boy. Jivaka became one of the best physicians cum surgeon of all times. He hailed Buddhism and became an ardent follower of Buddha. He constructed Amrabana Vihara for Buddha.

Jivakamravana : The great ancient physician *Jivaka* resided at a place away from *Venuvana.* He constructed a shrine for the master in the Mango-grove near his residence, so that, he could have the opportunity to meet the Blessed One more often. This was known as *Jivakamravana.*

Kapilpur : This place is also known on *Kapilavastu.* This was the capital of *Sakya* King *Suddodhana*, the father of *Gautama.* The Master was born and brought up here. The place is situated in Nepal.

King Sivi : King Sivi was a character of the Mahabharata. He was the son of king Ushinor. He was very famous for his charity and good conduct.

Kinnara : As per the Hindu and Buddhist mythology, Kinnara is a paradigmatic lover musician. The Kinnara couples never separate from each other and enjoy everlasting pleasure. They are perceived as half human (upper part) and half horse (lower part). They were said to be available in the Himalayan region.

Krittivas : Poet Krittivas Ojha translated the Sanskrit Ramayana into Bengali for the first time in the 15th Century AD.

Kolio : Like Sakya, Kolios were another tribesmen related to Buddha's clan.

Kunala Lake : As per the Jataka, this lake was situated on the eastern foothills of the Himalayan Mountains. The area possessed extremely charming scenic beauties of the nature. Green flowing streams came down the mountain slopes in rhythms. It was a magnificent lake with exotic fragrance of blooming blue lotuses, hundred-petal snow-white lilies etc. It was overrun and beautified by an array of heavenly trees, shrubs and creepers resounding with the cooing, warbling and whispering of the swans, ducks, geese and other aquatic birds. Monks, ascetics, top-ranking gods, demons, goblins, angelic beings etc, inhibited the place.

Kusinara : It was also known as *Kushinagara* or *Kusavati.* It is situated at 35 miles East of Gorakhpur. It was located in the *Malla* Kingdom. This is the place where the Blessed One had *Mahaparinirbana* and was cremated. He narrated *"Palasa-Jataka"* here while lying on the deathbed.

Kuru : He was a very powerful king of Mahabharata. He was the son of Tapati (daughter of the Sun) and king Sambaran. The Kaurava dynasty originated from him.

Kutagarsala : It was a part of *Mahavan* full of Saal trees, situated near *Vesali.* This was donated to the *Sangha* by a disciple named *Goshringi.* At times, Buddha used to stay here.

Magadha : Magadha was located in Bihar and was the capital of King *Bimbisara.* It was the hub of religious, political and cultural activities. Buddhism got deeply rooted in Magadha for ages.

Mahaparinirbana : A person, who attains Buddhahood after many rebirths, does not have to take further births on earth. On their death, they are said to have attained Mahaparinirbana.

Mongrel : It is an animal of mixed breed.

Narada : Narada was a son of Lord Vishnu. He remained a life bachelor. He was a music lover and used to play Veena. He used to be respected by all.

Nigrodharama or Banyan Park : This was a Banyan garden adjacent to *Kapilavastu.* Whenever the Blessed One visited *Kapilavastu*, he used to reside in this garden.

Odysseus : Odysseus is the main hero of the Greek epic Odyssey. He was the king of Ithaca, who participated in the long Trojan War and won. While returning home through the sea, he had to undergo lot of struggles as well as romantic experiences. Ultimately, he returned home after a long time and could unite with his family after settling right all troubles at home.

Ogress : A female man-eating monster.

Oracle of Delphi : It is believed to be the Devine revelation/forecast against specific questions regarding person/results of a forthcoming war etc. It was held at Pythia in Greece, where God Apollo used to send answers to the questions through his mouthpiece priestess Pythia.

Pachhekabuddha : They are a particular type of Buddhists. They themselves can even attain Nirvana but they do not possess the highest knowledge like Buddha. They do not preach any one and mostly like to stay incognito.

Paramour : An illicit lover of a married person.

Plateau : A plain land surrounded by mountains.

Purbarama : It was a place on the eastern fringe of *Sravasti.* Buddha's disciple *Visakha* bought this garden and constructed a monastery for the *Sangha.*

Quail : A bird of the partridge family.

Ravenously : To devour hungrily or greedily.

Rues : Trick to save oneself in case of danger.

Sacrilege : To spoil or impure some holy place or matter or person.

Sacristan : It is the person who performs odd but laborious jobs for a church like ringing bell, digging grave etc.

Sakka : The god king Indra is called Sakka also in Pali.

Sakya : Gautama Buddha's clan is called 'Sakya' clan

Samkassa : The modern name is *Sankisa*. It is situated in the district of Farukkabad on the bank of the river Kali. It is said that *Samkassa* was the capital of King *Kusaddhaja*, the brother of King *Janaka*.

Sangha : The religious society of Buddhists is called Sangha.

Shasta : The Lord Buddha is also called as 'Shasta'.

Shakuntala : The great Saint Viswamitra was well known for his dedication to meditation. He could achieve anything through meditation. Once he sat again for meditation. At this Indra got scared. He called upon the most beautiful nymph Menaka and ordered her to distract Viswamitra from meditation by seducing him. Menaka went to Viswamitra in transparent dresses. Suddenly, the wind also blew and she was left without any dress. Viswamitra forgot his meditation and welcomed Menaka as his companion. Menaka kept him immersed in sensual pleasures for about a year. After a year a baby girl was born to Menaka. She deserted the baby in the jungle and left for her abode in heaven. The newborn was surrounded by a group of vultures, who protected her. Saint Kanva discovered her. He took her to his hermitage and reared her as his own daughter.

Shrine of Agralava : This shrine was situated near the town of *Alavi*. *Alavi* was located on the way to *Rajagriha* from *Sravasti* at a distance of above 35 yojana (1 yojana = 7 miles) from the latter. This place was inhibited by a cannibal-*Yakkha* (demon) named *Alavak*, whom the Master transformed into a pious person.

The famous *Jetavana* monastery was situated adjacent to the city of *Sravasti.*

Sirens : They are the sea-creatures, who sing irresistible songs. They live in an island. Their songs lure the sailors, who ultimately meet their doom when they land in that island.

Sravasti : Sravasti was situated at modern "*Saheth-Maheth*" in the Utter Pradesh on the bank of the river *Aciravati* (modern Iravati).

It is said that, the city was founded by *Sravasta* (or *Savattha*, the son of "*Yuvanassa*").

As narrated in the preface or *Pachupannavatthu* of the "*Sarabha-Mriga Jataka*" (No. 483), the lord performed a great miraculous feat in *Sravasti.* This was performed to counter the wrong views of the *Tirthikas.* This was done in front of King *Prosenjit* (*Pasenadi*) and a huge assemblage of people.

Swamvar : It is a process by which the princesses were allowed to choose their own husbands. A big assembly of the eligible kings/princes were held at in the kingdom of the princess for this purpose and the groom used to be selected.

Normally some competition used to be held and the winner could win the bride. In the Ramayana, Rama could win Sita by breaking the strong bow named 'Haradhanu'. In the Mahabharata, Arjuna could win Draupadi by winning an arrow sports.

Tathagata : The Lord Buddha is also called as Tathagata.

Tirthika : They used to be a class of saints, who could

perform various types of supernatural activities like flying in the sky, walk on the water, staying above ground etc. These people did not have the knowledge of truth nor could preach the mankind.

Ussada hell : It is believed by most that there is a hell in that name, where all the sinners go. They have to undergo severe punishments for their misdeeds on the earth.

Vasistha : Vasistha was a great saint. Viswamitra had enmity towards him. He turned king Kalmaspad into a demon and got Vasistha's one hundred sons eaten up by the king. When the king tried to kill Vasistha's pregnant daughter in law, Vasistha sprinkled holy water on the king and restored him to normalcy.

Venuvana : This was a garden situated near *Rajagriha.* Buddha earlier used to reside at *Lasthivana*, which was situated at a distance of 12 Kms. from *Rajagriha.* King *Bimbisara* went there and became Buddha's disciple after listening to the narration of *Mahanarada-Kasspa Jataka* (544). He dedicated *Venuvana*, which was adjacent to his Kingdom to *Buddhist - Sangha*, so that he could visit the master often. Thereafter, this became the prime residence of the Lord till *Jetavana* monastery was donated by *Anatha-Pindika.*

After the assassination of *Bimbisara*, *Ajatasatru* constructed a huge monastery for *Devadatta* at *Gaya-sisa* near *Venuvana.*

From the statistics, we observe that, out of the 46 Jataka tales narrated at *Venuvana*, 34 Jatakas contains stories of *Devadatta's* wickedness in prior births.

Vidura : Vidura was the son of a maid and saint Vyas. He was actually the god of Dharma (religion). He was a prominent figure in the Mahabharata. He had vast knowledge and intelligence. He used to make running commentary to Dhritarashtra about day to day Kurushetra warfare.

Viswamitra : Viswamitra was the son of king Gadhi of Kanwakubja. One day he happened to reach the hermitage of Saint Vasistha. Vasistha welcomed him and treated him well. He had a Kamadhenu, a holy cow, which could produce anything asked from it. Vasistha got huge quantity of gems and jewellery from it and presented the same to king. King Viswamitra wanted to have the cow. Vasistha refused. The king's soldiers attacked Vasistha. The holy cow produced many armed soldiers from its body, who made the king's soldiers to run away. Viswamitra could understand that the Brahmins had more power than the Kshatriya kings. He performed meditation and could transform himself to a Brahmin saint from a king.

Vyas : He was the premarital son of Satyavati of Mahabharata. She was earlier known as Matsyagandha and was the daughter of a fisherman. She used to row ferry. One day Saint Parasar boarded her boat and had sex with her. As a result, Vyas was born. Unmarried Satyavati deserted him. Vyas later became a great saint and composed Mahabharata. Satyavati was later married to king Santanu. Queen Satyavati's sons Vichitravirya and Chitrangada died without keeping any heir to the throne. At the instruction of her mother, Vyas had sex with her two widowed daughter-in-laws; Amba and Ambalika and also with a maid. As a result, Dhritarashtra, Pandu and Vidura were born.

Water sprite : A fairy or monster who lives in a water-body.

Yaduvamsa : The dynasty of Lord Krishna is known as Yaduvamsa. At the end of the war of Kurushetra, no one from the Kuru dynasty could survive. Gandhari, the mother of the Kauravas held Sri Krishna responsible for the genocide and cursed him that his entire dynasty would be destroyed. And this happened to the Yaduvamsa.

Yoke : It is the heavy wooden bar, which is attached to the plough. The oxen ploughing the fields have to carry this heavy burden on their shoulders.

7.0 APPENDIX

7.1 Places of Narration

The Blessed one had narrated all the Jataka Tales at some place or the other. A tabulation of these places where the Jatakas were narrated is furnished herein below.

Sl. No.	Place of Narration	No. of occurrence
1	Jetavana	441
2	Venuvana (Bamboo - Grove)	46
3	Sravasti	6
4	Kutagarasala (Gabled chamber at the great Grove)	4
5	Kunala Lake	4
6	Ghosita Park near Kosambi	3
7	Shrine of Agralava near Alavi	3
8	Nigrodha-rama (Banyan Park at Kapilavastu)	3
9	Jivakamravana (Jivaka's Mango grove)	2
10	Badarika-rama (Badarika Monastery in Kosambi)	2
11	Magadha	2
12	On the death bed in Kusinara	2
13	At the gate of Samkassa town	2
14	Purba-rama (Eastern Garden)	2
15	Grijjhakuta (Vulture Peak) Parbata	2
16	Kapilapura or Kapilavastu	2
17	Anupriya Mango Grove	1

Sl. No.	Place of Narration	No. of occurrence
18	Ketaka-Vana near Nalaka-pana	1
19	On the way to Sravasti	1
20	In a village of Kosala Kingdom	1
21	Anjana-vana	1
22	Kundadhana-vana	1
23	On the bank of river Rohini	1
24	Patika-rama near Vesali	1
25	Desaka town in the Sumbha Country	1
26	Rajaka-rama monastery	1
27	Tapoda-rama near Rajagriha	1
28	Saketa	1
29	Subhaga-vana near Ukkattha	1
30	On the bank of the river Ganges	1
31	Dakshinagiri	1
32	Risipatana	1
33	Pugarama	1
34	Bhesakala-vana near Sumsumaragiri	1
35	Maddakuchhi deer park	1
36	Makhadevamra-vana	1
37	Lasthivana (Pleasure garden)	1
	Total :	547

Total number of places of narration is 37 as above.

7.2 Forms of Former Births

Bodhisattva had taken births in various forms before the ultimate one as *Gautama Buddha.* A tabulation of these different forms, as observed from the Jataka tales with the occurrences is appended below.

Sl. No.	Place of Narration	No. of occurrence
1	Ascetic	73
2	King	61
3	Minister	44
4	Tree Fairy	29
5	Treasurer	27
6	Teacher	27
7	*Sakka* (God Indra)	23
8	Prince	17
9	Brahmin	16
10	Wiseman	15
11	Priest	13
12	Merchant	13
13	Stag	12
14	Monkey	12
15	Lion	10
16	Bird	10
17	Mallard	9
18	Parrot	8
19	Elephant	7
20	Pigeon	6

Sl. No.	Place of Narration	No. of occurrence
21	Farmer / Gardener	5
22	Quail	5
23	Low-caste man	5
24	Bull	5
25	*Sasta (Buddha)*	4
26	God's son (spirit)	4
27	*Naga* (serpent)	4
28	Vulture	4
29	*Maha-Brahma*	3
30	Chaplain	3
31	Poor Householder	3
32	Lizard (Iguana)	3
33	Sea-sprite	3
34	Pupil	3
35	Youth	3
36	Horse	3
37	Fish	3
38	Peacock	3
39	Squire (Land-Lord)	2
40	Potter	2
41	House - holder	2
42	Lord - Justice	2
43	*Pachheka Buddha* (Highest form of Ascetic)	2
44	Spiritual Counsellor	2

Sl. No.	Place of Narration	No. of occurrence
45	Workman	2
46	Robber	2
47	Partridge	2
48	Crow	2
49	Rat	2
50	Woodpecker	2
51	*Garuda*	2
52	Jackal	2
53	Cock	2
54	Value Assessor	1
55	Doctor- Snake-bite	1
56	Drummer	1
57	Conch - blower	1
60	Barber	1
61	Tumbler (Beggar)	1
62	Musician	1
63	Forester	1
64	Fairy (forest)	1
65	Sprite of the air	1
66	Smith	1
67	Acrobat	1
68	Mariner	1
69	*Dharma* (The God of Religion)	1
70	Recluse	1
71	Carpenter	1

Sl. No.	Place of Narration	No. of occurrence
72	*Kinnara* (Fairy)	1
73	Hunter's son	1
74	Grass - sprite	1
75	*Buddha*	1
76	Dog	1
77	Marsh Crow	1
78	Frog	1
79	Winged Horse	1
80	Buffalo	1
81	Hare	1
82	Sow	1
83	Osprey	1
84	Gambler	1
85	Naked Ascetic	1
86	Priest's son	1
87	God	1
	Total :	**562**

7.3 Multiplicity of Births

A list of such multiple births is furnished below.

Sl. No.	No.	Jataka Jataka	Name of Births	No. of Form of Births
1	31	*Kulayaka*	2	*Brahmin, Sakka*
2	136	*Suvarnahamsa*	2	*Brahmin*, Mallard
3	291	*Bhadra-Ghata*	2	Treasurer, Priest
4	377	*Setaketu*	2	Teacher, Priest
5	390	*Madiyaka*	2	*Pacceka-Buddha*, Treasurer.
6	415	*Kulmashapinda*	2	Worker, King.
7	421	*Gangamala*	2	Worker, King
8	449	*Matta-Kundali*	2	Brahmin, God's son
9	458	*Udaya*	2	Prince, *Sakka*
10	498	*Chitta-Sambhuta*	4	*Chandala*, stag, bird, ascetic.
11	506	*Champeyya*	2	Poor house-holder, *Naga* (serpent)
12	524	*Samkhapala*	2	Prince, *Naga*.
13	541	*Nimi*	2	King (2)

Thus, the tally is as follows;

534 Jatakas X 1 birth = 534
12 Jatakas X 2 births = 24
1 Jataka X 4 births = 4

Total No. of births = 562

7.4 Places Referred to

In most of the Jataka tales, some place has been referred to, where the incidents were said to have taken place. A table of such places is appended below.

Sl. No.	Place of Narration	No. of occurrence
1	*Benares* (Varanasi)	441
2	*Mithila*	19
3	*Rajagaha* (Rajagriha)	11
4	*Indapatta* (Indraprastha)	7
5	*Magadha*	4
6	*Takshasila*	4
7	*Videha*	3
8	Thicket of forest near *Kunala* Lake in the *Himalayas*	3
9	*Uttara-panchala*	2
10	*Kasi*	2
11	*Himalayas*	2
12	*Panchala city*	2
13	City of *Aristapura*	2
14	*Anga* and *Maghdha*	2
15	*Kusavati (Kusinagara)*	2
16	Kingdom of *Seri*	1
17	Foot of a mountain	1
18	Lotus pond	1
19	*Kosala*	1

Sl. No.	Place of Narration	No. of occurrence
20	Dread thicket of a Jungle	1
21	*Sirisavasthu*, a Goblin town in Ceylon	1
22	*Bharu* Kingdom	1
23	*Kalinga* and *Assaka*	1
24	Mount *Dardara* in the *Himalayas*	1
25	*Ussada* Hell	1
26	The town of *Saketa* (*Oudh*) in *Kosala*	1
27	*Salindiya* Village (on the East of Rajagriha)	1
28	*Kashmira* and *Gandhara*	1
29	*Rourava* in *Sovira* Kingdom	1
30	*Grijjhakuta Parbata* (Vulture mountain)	1
31	Fig-grove in the *Himalayas*	1
32	*Molini* (The other name of *Benares*)	1
33	*Kosambi*	1
34	Certain unnamed place	1
35	City of *Asitanjana* in *Kamsa* district	1
36	City of *Surundha* (The other name of *Benares*)	1
37	City of *Ramma* (The other name of *Benares*)	1
38	*Bharu-kachha* Sea-port	1
39	Village of Carpenters (The other name *Benares*)	1

Sl. No.	Place of Narration	No. of occurrence
40	City of *Dantapura*	1
41	City of *Ujjeni*	1
42	Near Lake *Chaddanta* in the Himalayas	1
43	City of *Sudarsana* (The other name of *Benares*)	1
44	City of *Sakula*	1
45	City of *Pushpavati* (The other name of Benares)	1
46	City of *Brahmavardana* (The other name of Benares)	1
47	City of *Jetuttara* (near *Jetavana*)	1
48	*Nalaka-pana* village near *Ketakavana*	1
49	Tank of *Jetavana*	1
50	Forest, adjoining the Border of *Magadha*	1
51	Hamlet of *Machala* in the *Magadha*	1
	Total :	**543**

Thus, we observe that the total number of places referred to is 543 with Benares topping the list with a score of 441 followed by *Mithila* and *Rajagriha* with scores 19 and 11 respectively. Balance places have single digit scores. Total number of places count to 51.

Out of balance 547-543=4 cases, incidences of 3 nos. Jatakas have taken place in the early inception of the world and for the lone left out one, no place has been specified.

It is interesting to know that "*Benares*" also had the following seven additional names.

1. *Molini*
2. *Surundha nagara*
3. *Ramma nagara*
4. The Villages of Carpenters
5. *Sudarshana nagara*
6. *Brahmavardhana*
7. *Pushpavati*

7.5 Reigning Kings

In most of the Jataka tales, the names of the Kings reigning at the time of incidences have been mentioned. Summary of the statistics is furnished below.

Sl. No.	Name of the Reigning Kings	No. of Occurrence
1.	*Brahmadatta*	399
2.	*Videha*	14
3.	*Magadha*	8
4.	*Dhananjaya*	6
5.	*Panchala*	4
6.	*Bodhisattva*	3
7.	*Sivi*	3
8.	*Maha-Janaka*	3
9.	*Kasi*	2
10.	King of *Gandhara*	2
11.	*Assaka*	2
12.	*Mahasammata*	2
13.	*Suruci*	2
14.	*Kalinga*	2
15.	Parrot King	2
16.	*Kosambika*	2
17.	*Koravya*	2
18.	*Makhadeva*	2
19.	*Bharu*	2

Sl. No.	Name of the Reigning Kings	No. of Occurrence
20.	*Sama*	1
21.	*Susima*	1
22.	*Yasapani*	1
23.	*Maha-Pingala*	1
24.	*Vissasena*	1
25.	*Suradardara*	1
26.	*Kalabu*	1
27.	*Mahapratapa*	1
28.	*Tamba*	1
29.	*Senaka*	1
30.	*Mandava*	1
31.	*Janaka*	1
32.	*Dalhadharma*	1
33.	*Bharata*	1
34.	*Buddha-Kassapa*	1
35.	*Maha-Kamsa*	1
36.	*Sarbadatta*	1
37.	*Dasaratha*	1
38.	*Usinara*	1
39.	*Sadhina*	1
40.	*Avanti*	1
41.	*Bahuputraka*	1
42.	*Bhallatiya*	1

Sl. No.	Name of the Reigning Kings	No. of Occurrence
43.	*Renu*	1
44.	*Anga*	1
45.	*Esukari*	1
46.	*Okkaka*	1
47.	*Manoja*	1
48.	*Sakula*	1
49.	*Samyama*	1
50.	*Ekaraja*	1
51.	*Angati*	1
52.	*Kosala*	1
	Total	***495.***

Thus, we find that 52 kings are named in all, of which, *Brahmadatta* tops the list with a score of 399.

7.6 Repetition of Titles

Repetition of Titles of the Jatakas is also worth noting. While, the stories of some of the Jatakas having the same title are similar, there are also variations in the stories among the Jatakas bearing the same title. A summary of such phenomenon follows.

Sl.No.	Title	Jātaka No.	Short Commentary
1	*Kuranga-mriga Jataka*	21	A hunter threw fruits from a tree to lure a deer within aim. The deer detected the artifice and escaped.
		206	A woodpecker and a tortoise rescued their deer friend from the trap of a hunter.
2	*Kanha Jataka*	29	A bull drew 500 carts to earn livelihood for his poor mistress.
		440	An ascetic made wise choice of boons offered by *Sakka*.
3	*Machha Jataka*	34	A fish, blinded by passion for wife was caught by fishermen but was set free by a Brahmin.
		75	A pious fish saved his kins from draught.
		216	Similar to *Jataka* No 34.

Sl.No.	Title	Jātaka No.	Short Commentary
4	*Vartaka Jataka*	35	A baby quail engulfed in Jungle fire protected itself by the power of truth.
		118	A quail caught by a fowler protected itself by starvation.
		394	A quail advised a crow how to attain healthy physique in spite of living on ordinary foods.
5.	*Tittira Jataka*	37	A partridge, a monkey and an elephant, living together, decided seniority by recalling their memories.
		117	A talkative man was killed by a jaundiced ascetic. A partridge was killed for excessive chatter.
		319	A decoy partridge was perturbed with scruples of conscience.
		438	A wicked ascetic killed a learned partridge, which was avenged by a lion and a tiger.
6	*Baka Jataka*	38	A wicked crane, pretending to be a

Sl.No.	Title	Jātaka No.	Short Commentary
			saviour, devoureded fishes of a pond. A wise crab avenged this by killing the crane.
		236	A crane intending to catch fish, pretended dreaming. A wise fish cautioned others of the wicked motive.
7	*Kapota Jataka*	42	A greedy crow befriended a pigeon to steal food from a kitchen. He was tortured to death by the cook.
		375	Same as *Jataka* No.42.
8	*Aramadusaka Jataka*	46	Monkeys deployed for watering trees uprooted them to measure roots to assess requirement of water.
		268	Same as *Jataka* No.46.
9	*Durmedha Jataka*	50	A king stopped sacrifice of living beings.
		122	Being jealous of his elephant, a king tried to kill him by asking to perform dangerous tasks. The elephant performed all these tasks and flew away.

Sl.No.	Title	Jātaka No.	Short Commentary
10	*Anabhirati Jataka*	65	Women common to all.
		185	A pupil forgot Vedas after getting married.
11	*Saketa Jataka*	68	An old Brahmin couple claimed lord Buddha as their son.
		237	Same as *Jataka* No.68.
12	*Mitrvinda Jataka*	82.	A jealous recluse had to reborn many times and underwent extreme sufferings for his evil deeds.
		104	Same as *Jataka* No. 82.
		369	Same as *Jataka* No. 82.
13	*Kalakarni Jataka*	83	A good heart and not the name is the identity of a person.
		192	A wise courtier of a king is attempted to be harassed by his four unwise and evil colleagues several times. The wise courtier crossed all hurdles successfully.
		382	A good merchant settled superiority between the goddesses of good and evil fortunes.
14	*Sila-mimamsha Jataka*	86	In order to test the price of esteem, a Brahmin stole.

Sl.No.	Title	Jātaka No.	Short Commentary
		290	Similar to *Jataka* No. 86.
		305	A teacher tested his pupils' virtue and married off his daughter to the honest one.
		330	A man learnt the power of virtue from a hawk and a maid.
		362	Similar to *Jataka* No. 86.
15	*Kuta-vanijya Jataka*	98.	A rogue hid in a hollow tree to umpire between two disputees as a tree sprite. A fire lighted at the bottom of the tree exposed the cheat.
		218	A man tried to cheat his friend of the ploughshare deposited with him. The friend exposed the guilt in an intelligent way.
16	*Srigala Jataka*	113.	A Brahmin, lured by a jackal led him out of the city safely but got indignities in return in lieu of treasure.
		142	To catch a jackal, a man pretended to be dead. The clever jackal detected the motive and ran away to safety.

Sl.No.	Title	Jātaka No.	Short Commentary
		148	A greedy jackal ate his way in to the carcass of a dead elephant and got trapped inside. With great difficulty he came out loosing all his hair.
		152	A wise young lion protected his sister from a clever jackal, who proposed to marry her.
17	*Amra Jataka*	124	During a severe draught, a hermit worked hard to provide water for the beasts. The beasts reciprocated the gesture by fetching mango and other fruits for him.
		474	A man learnt the charm of growing mango during the off-season. The charm vanished when he disowned his low-caste teacher.
18	*Kaushiki - Jataka*	130	Pretended illness of a wife is cured by a stick and filthy food.
		226	An owl was devoured by Crows when he came out of nest untimely.
		470	A rich miser was converted into a wise

Sl.No.	Title	Jātaka No.	Short Commentary
			ascetic and he enjoyed the heavenly pleasure thereafter.
19	*Godha Jataka*	138	A wicked hermit tried in the vain to catch a lizard (Iguana) for making a meal out of him.
		141	A chameleon betrayed a tribe of iguanas to a hunter.
		325	Same as *Jataka* No.138.
		333	A king ate a roasted lizard himself and told the queen that it had run away. He was convicted for his ingratitude to his wife.
20	*Kaka Jataka*	140	Angered by wicked behaviour of a crow, a king's chaplain tried to kill all the crows, which were saved by their leader.
		146	A hen crow having been drowned in the sea, other crows tried to bale the sea out with their beaks.
		395	A greedy crow befriended a pigeon to steal food from a kitchen.

Sl.No.	Title	Jātaka No.	Short Commentary
			He was ridiculed to death by the cook.
21	*Radha Jataka*	145	Two parrots narrated a Brahmin the misconduct of his wife during his absence.
		198	Similar to *Jataka* No.145. Here, one of the parrots was killed by the wife when he tried to preach her good lessons.
22	*Rajovada Jataka*	151	Two kings of equal status and power met from opposite directions on a narrow road. The superiority of the kings was debated and the superior was given the way.
		334	An ascetic told a king that the fruits in a country became sweet or bitter depending upon the wisdom of the ruling king. The king checked the same and found it true.
23	*Uraga Jataka*	154	A *garuda* chased a serpent which took the form of a jewel and hid in the robe of an ascetic and saved itself.

Sl.No.	Title	Jātaka No.	Short Commentary
		354	A Brahmin family kept their cool even when they lost their only son.
24	*Susima Jataka*	163	A chaplain's son travelled 2000 leagues, learnt 3 Vedas and elephant lore in one day and performed the elephant festival.
		411	A king became an ascetic on being shown a grey hair by his queen consort.
25	*Griddha Jataka*	164	Pet vultures of a merchant stole various items from other citizens and brought those to the courtyard of the merchant.
		399	A good young vulture was set free form trap by a hunter.
		427	A vulture perished attempting to venture a flight too high.
26	*Dardara Jataka*	172	A jackal, posed as a lion was identified by his voice.
		304	Two brothers were exiled from the kingdom for 3 years due to misdeeds of the younger.

Sl.No.	Title	Jātaka No.	Short Commentary
27	*Kachhapa Jataka*	178	A tortoise had to breathe his last because he did not leave his home in draught.
		215	A tortoise while being carried in air by two geese tried to speak and fell on ground and died.
		273	A monkey insulted a tortoise and was punished.
28	*Mitramitra Jataka*	197	An ascetic kept a young orphaned elephant and was killed by him when the elephant grew up in size.
		473	How to distinguish between a friend and a foe.
29	*Somadatta Jataka*	21	A foolish man offered his own ox to the king instead of asking for one.
		410	An ascetic became very sad when a young elephant died. He was consoled by God Indra.
30	*Dharmaddhaja Jataka*	220	Impossible tasks were set to a good man, who performed those all with the help of God Indra.

Sl.No.	Title	Jātaka No.	Short Commentary
		384	A deceptive crow posed as a holy bird and ate eggs of other birds. This was detected and he was killed.
31	*Kapi Jataka*	250	A monkey posed as an ascetic, was identified and driven away.
		404	Foolish monkeys staying near enemy's abode died. Wise monkeys went away and were saved.
32	*Duta Jataka*	260	A man earned a meal by calling himself his belly's meassanger.
		478	A pupil collected his teacher's withal from the king by starvation.
33	*Sujata Jataka*	269	A king taught his badmouth mother a lesson from the voice of a jay and a cuckoo.
		306	Daughter of a fruit seller became a queen and almost lost her position due to her unwarranted pride.
		352	A father is cured of inordinate grief by feigned madness of his son.

Sl.No.	Title	Jātaka No.	Short Commentary
34	*Palasa Jataka*	307	A Brahmin paid honour to a Tree Sprite and is rewarded by discovery of a buried treasure.
		370	A Judas tree was destroyed by the parasitic growth of a Banyan shoot.
35	*Ghata Jataka*	355	A king was taken prisoner and tortured but through his patience under sufferings, he won his enemy to repentance.
		454	A girl, kept prisoner in a tower, gave birth to ten sons, who defeated the king but finally perished.
36	*Kukkuta Jataka*	383	A cat failed to deceive a cock.
		448	A falcon tried to befriend a foul, which could not be deceived.
37	*Mahakapi Jataka*	407	A monkey saved his brother at the cost of his own life.
		516	A man, searching for his oxen, lost in the forest and was rescued by a monkey. Later, he tried to kill the monkey and got smitten by leprosy.

Sl.No.	Title	Jātaka No.	Short Commentary
38	*Chakravaka Jataka*	434	A crow wanted to attain the beauty of ruddy goose but could not do so because of his food habits.
		451	Same as *Jataka* No. 434.

From the foregoing, we observe that 38 Nos. titles have been used in 93 stories.

7.7 Stories Revisited

We observe that some of the Jataka tales bear close resemblance with other Jatakas. In some such tales there are minor changes in the characters or stories. In some cases, both the stories are almost same. Some Jataka tales are themselves part of another Jataka.

The first part or 'Preface' of a Jataka tale is called *Pachupannavasthu*, which precedes the "Former birth story". There are similarities in the *Pachupannavasthu* of various Jatakas also. In this chapter, we shall go through resemblances only.

Sl.No.	Title	Jātaka No.	Short Commentary
1(i) (ii)	*Devadharma Jataka* *Dasaratha Jataka*	6 461	There is a part similarity in these two Jatakas. In both the cases, the princes had to leave the kingdoms and stay in the forest due to conspiracy hatched by the wicked stepmother.
2(i) (ii)	*Gramani Jataka* *Samvara Jataka*	8 462	In both the stories, the Prince ascended to the throne by the virtue of his modesty and wisdom.
3(i) (ii) (iii) (iv)	*Makhadeva Jataka* *Susima Jataka* *Chulla-Sutasoma* *Nimi Jataka*	9 411 525 541	In all the stories, the kings renounced the throne and became an ascetic after detecting a grey hair on their heads.

Sl.No.	Title	Jātaka No.	Short Commentary
4(i) (ii)	*Nigrodhamriga Jataka* *Nandikamriga Jataka*	12 385	The king deer not only saved his brotherhood, also but all other animals from being slaughtered.
5(ii) (ii)	*Mahilamuka Jataka* *Giridanta Jataka*	26 184	An elephant became a rogue after listening to thieves. It killed its mentor. A good horse tried to imitate its lame trainer. In both cases, the animals were restored to normalcy on removal of the causes of the influences.
6(i) (ii)	*Munika Jataka* *Saluka Jataka*	30 286	In both the stories, an ox envied gracious meals being fed to a lazy pig, which was ultimately slaughtered on the occasion of marriage of the owner's daughter. The names of the pigs in *Jataka* 30 & 286 are *Munika* and *Saluka* respectively.
7(i) (ii) (iii) (iv) (v)	*Loshaka Jataka* *Mitravinda Jataka* *Mitravinda Jataka* *Mitrarinda Jataka* *Chatudvara Jataka*	41 82 104 369 439	A jealous recluse had to reborn many times and underwent extreme sufferings for his evil deeds. All Jatakas narrate

Sl.No.	Title	Jātaka No.	Short Commentary
			the same story or part thereof.
8(i) (ii) (iii) (iv) (v)	*Kapota Jataka* *Lola Jataka* *Rucira Jataka* *Kapota Jataka* *Kaka Jataka*	42 274 275 375 395	A greedy crow befriended a pigeon and stole food from a kitchen. He was ridiculed to death by the cook. All Jatakas bear the same story.
9(i)	*Venuka Jataka*	43	A person reared a snake and was killed by it.
(ii)	*Indrasamanagotra Jataka*	161	A person reared an elephant and was killed by it.
(iii)	*Mitramitra Jataka*	197	- do-
10(i)	*Masaka Jataka*	44	A stupid son killed his father while trying to kill a mosquito.
(ii)	*Rohini Jataka*	45	A stupid daughter killed her mother while trying to kill a fly.
11(i) (ii)	*Aramadusaka Jataka* *Aramadusaka Jataka*	46 268	Monkeys employed to water trees in a garden, uprooted those to assess requirement of water for each tree.
12(i) (ii)	*Machha Jataka* *Machha Jataka*	34 216	A fish blinded by passion for wife was caught by fishermen and was killed.
13(i) (ii)	*Mahasilava Jataka* *Shreyo Jataka*	51 282	All stories are similar. A king won his enemy to

Sl.No.	Title	Jātaka No.	Short Commentary
(iii) (iv) (v)	*Ekaraja Jataka* *Manikundala Jataka* *Ghata Jataka*	303 351 355	repentance by his patience under sufferings
14(i) (ii)	*Chulajanaka Jataka* *Mahajanaka Jataka*	52 539	*Jataka* No. 52 is a part of *Jataka* No. 539
15(i) (ii) (iii)	*Phala Jataka* *Kimpakka Jataka* *Gulmika Jataka*	54 85 366	Greedy travellers ate poisonous fruits in defiance to the warning of their leader.
16(i) (ii) (iii) (iv)	*Vanarenda Jataka* *Sisusumara Jataka* *Kumbhira Jataka* *Vanara Jataka*	57 208 224 342	Jatakas 57 & 224 are same. Other two are slightly different. A crocodile tried to kill a monkey, who outwitted the former and saved his own life.
17(i) (ii)	*Bherivada Jataka* *Samkhadharma Jataka*	59 60	A foolish drummer (59) /conch blower (60) attracted attention of robbers by beating drum / blowing conch at a wrong time.
18(i) (ii)	*Durajana Jataka* *Anabhirati Jataka*	64 65	Both the stories are same and narrate the sinful character of a wife.
19(i) (ii) (iii)	*Mridulakshana Jataka* *Samkalpa Jataka* *Harita Jataka*	66 251 431	A hermit fell in love with the queen and finally got cured. All the three stories are similar.

Sl.No.	Title	Jātaka No.	Short Commentary
20(i) (ii)	*Saketa Jataka* *Saketa Jataka*	68 237	A Brahmin couple claimed Buddha their son. Both the stories are similar.
21(i) (ii)	*Kuddala Jataka* *Hastipala Jataka*	70 509	Both stories are similar. These are. about people who left worldly attachments and became hermits.
22(i) (ii)	*Silavanaga Jataka* *Saradanta Jataka*	72 514	In both the stories, an elephant voluntarily allows a poacher to cut his trunks. Jataka 514 is an extension of Jataka No. 72.
23(i) (ii) (iii)	*Mahasapna Jataka* *Louhakumbhi Jataka* *Asthasabda Jataka*	77 314 418	All the stories are similar. The king got frightened on hearing peculiar sounds in sleep. Brahmins arrange to sacrifice animals, while *Bodhisattva* explained true reasons and prevented animal slaughtering.
24(i) (ii)	*Arthassadvara Jataka* *Ekapada Jataka*	84 238	Both stories are similar. A boy asked philosophical question to his father, who answered those.
25(i) (ii)	*Nandivisala Jataka* *Sarambha Jataka*	28 88	By abusing a bull, the owner lost his bet but

Sl.No.	Title	Jātaka No.	Short Commentary
			regained by praising him. Both the stories are same.
26(i) (ii) (iii)	*Silamimamsa Jataka* -Do- -Do-	86 290 362	In order to test the virtue of esteem, a Brahmin stole. All the stories are same.
27(i) (ii) (iii)	*Akritagna Jataka* *Asampadana Jataka* *Hri Jataka*	90 131 363	A merchant helped his merchant friend in need. But the friend did not reciprocate the same during the distress of his benefactor. All stories are similar but *Jatakas* 90 & 363 are same.
28(i) (ii)	*Tailapatra Jataka* *Panchagaru Jataka*	96 132	A Prince won a kingdom by resisting the fascinations of lovely Ogresses. Both stories are same.
29(i) (ii) (iii) (iv)	*Parosahasra Jataka* *Parosata Jataka* *Dhyanasodhana Jataka* *Chandrabha Jataka*	99 101 134 135	An ascetic described his spiritual attainments to his disciples in his dying statement, which was not understood by his pupils excepting one. All stories are same.
30(i) (ii)	*Parnika Jataka* *Seggu Jataka*	102 217	To test his daughter's virtue, father offered to make love with her. Both stories are same.

Sl.No.	Title	Jātaka No.	Short Commentary
31(i) (ii) (iii) (iv) (v) (vi)	*Udanchani Jataka* *Aranya Jataka* *Chulla-Narada Jataka* *Haridraga Jataka* *Alambusa Jataka* *Nalinika Jataka*	106 348 477 435 523 526	A young hermit is seduced by a girl. The hermit came back to senses when he understood the reality. All the stories are similar.
32(i) (ii) (iii) (iv)	*Sarbasamhara Prashna Jataka* *Gardabha Prashna Jataka* *Amaradevi Prashna Jataka* *Maha Unmarga Jataka*	110 111 112 546	The first three Jatakas are part of the 4th Jataka.
33(i) (ii) (iii)	*Durbaca Jataka* *Mrigalopa Jataka* *Griddha Jataka*	116 381 427	An acrobat tried to jump beyond the limit and died. A vulture tried to fly above his limits and perished.
34(i) (ii)	*Bandhanamoksha Jataka* *Mahapaduma Jataka*	120 472	A queen committed adultery with footmen but failed to do so with chaplain. The queen tried to seduce her stepson but failed.
35(i) (ii)	*Katahaka Jataka* *Kalanduka Jataka*	125 127	A slave married a rich girl forging his master's signature. His arrogance to his wife was subdued by a verse revealing his identity.

Sl.No.	Title	Jātaka No.	Short Commentary
36(i) (ii) (iii) (iv) (v) (vi) (vii)	*Birala Jataka* *Agnika Jataka* *Godha Jataka* *Srigala Jataka* *Romaka Jataka* *Godha Jataka* *Dharmaddhaja Jataka*	128 129 138 142 277 325 384	In Jatakas 128 & 129, jackal ate rats pretending to be a saint. In 138 & 325, an ascetic tried to catch lizards for eating. In 142, a man tried to make a meal of a jackal. In 277, a saint tried to catch a pigeon for eating. In 384, a crow ate eggs & chicks of other birds pretending to be a saint.
37(i) (ii)	*Kaka Jataka* *Kapi Jataka*	140 404	In Jataka 140, a crow brought about devastation to his brethren by his misdeeds. In Jataka 404, the crow is replaced by monkey.
38(i) (ii) (iii) (iv)	*Virocana Jataka* *Viraka Jataka* *Kandagalaka Jataka* *Jambuka Jataka*	143 204 210 335	All tales are similar. In Jatakas 143 & 335, a jackal died trying to imitate a lion. In 204, a crow perished trying to imitate a marsh- crow. Similar was the fate of a bird trying to act like a woodpecker.
39(i) (ii)	Lang*ustha Jataka* *Sangstava Jataka*	144 162	In two different incidents, ascetics found the god of fire useless and gave up worshipping him.

Sl.No.	Title	Jātaka No.	Short Commentary
40(i) (ii)	*Radha Jataka* *Radha Jataka*	145 198	Two pet parrots kept vigil on the unchaste wife during her husband's absence and informed the later on return. In 198, a parrot was killed while trying to preach the unchaste wife.
41(i) (ii)	*Pushparakta Jataka* *Kama-Vilapa Jataka*	147 297	To fulfill wife's unjust wishes, a man tried to steal from King's Conservatory and was condemned to death. Both the stories are similar.
42(i) (ii)	*Uraga Jataka* *Nakula Jataka*	154 165	An ascetic established friendship between two arch-rivals, a garuda and a serpant in 154 and between mongoose and snake in 165.
43(i) (ii) (iii)	*Guna Jataka* *Tiritavachha Jataka* *Mahaassaroha Jataka*	157 259 302	In Jataka 157, a lion made friendship and showed gratitude to a jackal's family, who saved his life. In Jatakas 259 & 302, a king showed similar gesture to a poor countryman.
44(i) (ii)	*Mayura Jataka* *Mahamayura Jataka*	159 491	In these stories, a holy golden peacock / goose

Sl.No.	Title	Jātaka No.	Short Commentary
(iii) (iv) (v)	*Hamsa Jataka* *Chulla-hamsa Jataka* *Maha-hamsa Jataka*	502 533 539	was taken prisoner but later let off. All stories are similar but some are identical.
45(i) (ii) (iii)	*Vinilaka Jataka* *Simha-kosthuka Jataka* *Kachhapa* Jataka	160 188 215	There are partial similarities between 160 & 188 and between 160 & 215. In 160, an offspring of a goose and a crow is deserted by his father for his arrogance. In Jataka 188, similar is the fate of a mongrel of a lion and a jackal. In 160 & 215 a bird and a tortoise are flown in the air by two swans holding a stick in their beaks
46(i) (ii)	*Kakantaka Jataka* *Mahaunmarga Jataka*	170 546	*Jataka* No. 170 is a part of *Jataka* No. 546.
47(i) (ii)	*Markata Jataka* *Kapi Jataka*	173 250	Both the stories are same. A monkey disguised as an ascetic was identified and driven out.
48(i) (ii)	*Sri-Kalakarni Jataka* *Mahaunmarga Jataka*	192 546	*Jataka* No. 192 is a part of *Jataka* No. 546.

Sl.No.	Title	Jātaka No.	Short Commentary
49(i) (ii)	*Parbatupatthara Jataka* *Khanti-Varnana Jataka*	195 225	Both the stories are similar. *An* intriguer courtier was condoned and made to amend his ways.
50(i) (ii) (iii) (iv) (v) (vi)	*Assaka Jataka* *Matarodana Jataka* *Sujata Jataka* *Uraga Jataka* *Mrigapotaka Jataka* *Somadatta Jataka*	207 317 352 354 372 410	All the stories are similar in nature. These demonstrate that, becoming aggrieved due to death of near and dear ones is meaningless.
51(i) (ii) (iii) (iv)	*Puta-Bhakta Jataka* *Sutyaga Jataka* *Godha Jataka* *Sambla Jataka*	223 320 332 519	All stories are similar. Ungrateful king showed ingratitude to his devoted wife.
52(i) (ii)	*Kamanita Jataka* *Kama Jataka*	228 467	A prince, who renounced the throne, later became greedy and was cured by Sakka (Indra)
53(i) (ii)	*Palayi Jataka* *Dutiya Palayi Jataka*	228 230	A king invaded a kingdom but got frightened and ran away.
54(i) (ii)	*Upana Jataka* *Guttila Jataka*	231 243	A pupil tried to outdo his teacher but was humbled by the latter. The teachers were a chaplain and a musician in 231 & 243 respectively.
55(i) (ii)	*Vaka Jataka* *Vaka Jataka*	236 300	A crane (236) and a wolf (300) pretended to be

Sl.No.	Title	Jātaka No.	Short Commentary
			pious to catch their prey but were exposed.
56(i) (ii)	*Jarudpana Jataka* *Maha-vanijya Jataka*	256 493	Some merchants found treasure from a well (256) / a tree (493). But greed drove them to destroy the source and they were ultimately killed.
57(i) (ii)	*Chullapralobhana Jataka* *Mahapralobhana Jataka*	263 507	A woman-hater prince was lured by a woman but he ultimately renounced the world. Both the stories are same.
58(i) (ii)	*Mahapranada Jataka* *Suruchi Jataka*	264 489	Both the stories are same. It's about a pious prince.
59(i) (ii)	*Vardhakisukara Jataka* *Takshaka-sukara Jataka*	283 492	An intelligent boar was reared by a carpenter. He outwitted a dangerous tiger and a false ascetic and killed them.
60(i) (ii)	*Sri Jataka* *Nigrodha Jataka*	284 445	Both the stories are similar and partially same. By eating cock's meat a man became king.
61(i) (ii)	*Jambu-khadaka Jataka* *Anta Jataka*	294 295	A fox flattered a crow to eat fruits. A crow flatters a fox to eat corpse of a cow.
62(i) (ii)	*Sajhya Jataka* *Darimukha Jataka*	310 378	All the stories are similar. A prince's friend

Sl.No.	Title	Jātaka No.	Short Commentary
(iii) (iv)	*Lomakassapa Jataka* *Sonaka Jataka*	433 529	renounced worldly temptations and became an Ascetic.
63(i) (ii)	*Khantivadi Jataka* *Culladharmapala Jataka*	313 358	In 313, a king being jealous of an ascetic's holiness, mutilated his body and killed him. The king was cast to hell. In 358 a king did the same to his own infant son.
64(i) (ii)	*Kanavera Jataka* *Sulasa Jataka*	318 419	Both the stories are similar. In 318, a courtesan rescued a Robber condemned to death by betraying her lover. The robber finally tried to kill her and deserted her. In 419, the courtesan finally killed the robber, who intended to kill her.
65(i) (ii)	*Kakavati Jataka* *Sushroni Jataka*	327 360	Both the stories are same. A roc carried away his friendly king's wife to his island for pleasure. Being outwitted by the king's minstrel, he retuned her.
66(i) (ii)	*Tuhsa Jataka* *Musika Jataka*	338 373	Both the stories are similar. By reciting a spell at critical moments, a king foiled attempts by his son to murder him.

Sl.No.	Title	Jātaka No.	Short Commentary
67(i) (ii) (iii)	*Kandari Jataka* *Chulla-kunala Jataka* *Kunala Jataka*	341 464 536	*Jatakas* 341 and 464 are part of *Jataka* No. 536
68(i) (ii)	*Sandhibheda Jataka* *Varnaroha Jataka*	349 361	In 349, a wicked jackal created fatal rift between a bull and a lion, who were friends. In 361, a jackal made similar attempt between a lion and a tiger but failed.
69(i) (ii) (iii)	*Devataprashna Jataka* *Khadyotapanaka Jataka* *Maha-unmarga Jataka*	350 364 546	*Jataka* Nos 350 & 364 are part of *Jataka* No. 546
70(i) (ii)	*Sarika Jataka* *Takasara Jataka*	367 368	A village doctor wanted to harm a boy with snake bite but got killed himself. Both the stories are similar. 368 has a little addition over 367.
71(i) (ii)	*Dighitakosala Jataka* *Kosambi Jataka*	371 428	A Prince spared the life of a king, who had killed his father and won him to repentance.
72(i) (ii)	*Setketu Jataka* *Uddalaka Jataka*	377 487	Both the stories are almost similar. A Brahmin boy tried to establish his spiritual superiority to the king but failed.

Sl.No.	Title	Jātaka No.	Short Commentary
73(i) (ii)	*Srikalakarni Jataka* *Sudhabhojana Jataka*	382 535	In 382, a Merchant decided superiority between two goddesses. In 535, superiority between four goddesses is decided.
74(i) (ii)	*Kukkuta Jataka* *Kukkuta Jataka*	383 448	Both the stories are similar. In 383, a cat tried to befriend a foul to eat him, but failed. In 488, the cat is replaced by a falcon.
75(i) (ii) (iii)	*Vartaka Jataka* *Chakravaka Jataka* *Chakravaka Jataka*	394 434 451	In 394, a greedy crow tried to attain the physique of the quail and was told that his food habits and behaviour were responsible for his look. In the other two, the quail is replaced by a pair of ruddy geese.
76(i) (ii)	*Katyayani Jataka* *Takkala Jataka*	417 446	In both the stories, an ungrateful son drives out mother from home (417) / attempts to bury father(446) at the instigation of his wicked wife. Finally, the son realised his mistake.
77(i) (ii)	*Mahasuka Jataka* *Chullasuka Jataka*	429 430	Both the stories are same. A grateful parrot refused to desert a barren fig tree.

Sl.No.	Title	Jātaka No.	Short Commentary
78 (i) (ii)	*Krishna Jataka* *Akirti Jataka*	440 480	Both the stories are similar. A person inherited abundant wealth, which he renounced and became an ascetic. God Indra gave him boons.
79(i) (ii)	*Chatusposadhika Jataka* *Vidhurapandita Jataka*	441 545	*Jataka* 441 is a part of *Jataka* No.545.
80(i) (ii)	*Bhuriprashna Jataka* *Unmarga Jataka*	452 546	*Jataka* No. 452 is a part of *Jataka* No. 546.
81(i) (ii)	*MendakaprashnaJataka* *Unmarga Jataka*	471 546	*Jataka* No. 471 is a part of *Jataka* No. 546.
82(i) (ii)	*Ruru Jataka* *Rohanta-mriga Jataka*	482 501	Both stories are similar. A golden deer preached the queen.
83(i) (ii)	*Srimanda Jataka* *Mahaunmarga Jataka*	500 546	*Jataka* 500 is a part of *Jataka* No. 546
84(i) (ii) (iii)	*Champeyya Jataka* *Samkhapala Jataka* *Bhuridatta Jataka*	506 524 543	Some parts of all the stories are similar. A *Naga* king, while performing holy rites, was caught and tortured but he gained freedom.
85(i) (ii)	*Panchapandita Jataka* *Mahaunmarga Jataka*	508 546	*Jataka* No. 805 is a part of - *Jataka* No. 546.

Sl.No.	Title	Jātaka No.	Short Commentary
86(i) (ii)	*Ayogriha Jataka* *Jayadwisa Jataka*	510 513	There is similarity in the 1st part of both the stories.
87(i) (ii)	*Udakarakshasa Jataka* *Mahaunmarga Jataka*	517 546	*Jataka* No. 517 is a part of *Jataka* No.546

From the above tabulation, we observe that, there are 87 Nos. of significant similarities / repetitions of stories involving 216 Nos Jataka stories. Apart from these, there are many more partial similarities among various stories, which have not been accounted for since the similarities are not significant in nature.

7.8 Important Occasions

There were a few note-worthy occasions, which served as backgrounds for the Tathagata to bless the mankind with a Jataka tale. Some of such notable occasions are enlisted below.

Sl.No.	Title	Jātaka No.	Short Commentary
1	*Vartaka Jataka*	35	Once the Lord with the Brethren were surrounded by aggressive jungle fire. But the flame abruptly got extinguished at a little distance away from the Lord, saving the lives of all miraculously.
2(i) (ii) (iii)	*Briksha-dharma Jataka* *Spandana Jataka* *Kunala Jataka*	74 475 536	Once the two tribesmen-*Sakya* and *Koliya* of the Master's Kinsmen prepared for a war against each other over a dispute on distribution of the water of *Rohini* River. The Master narrated these tales and brought amity between the two warring groups.
3	*Machha Jataka*	75	Once there was a severe drought in *Kosala* due to lack of rain. The Blessed one stood on the steps of the Jetavana Tank and asked Ananda to get him

Sl.No.	Title	Jātaka No.	Short Commentary
			bath- robe. A heavy shower followed till the tank got filled up. Thereupon the Lord narrated the tale.
4(i) (ii) (iii)	*Mahasapna Jataka* *Lohakumbhi Jataka* *Asthasabda Jataka*	77 31 418	In all the three cases, the king of *Kosala* was horrorified by terrible sounds / dreams. Buddha explained the meanings of those and then narrated the tales.
5(i) (ii)	*Mahasudarsana Jataka* *Palasa Jataka*	95 307.	The Blessed one, stretched on the death bed at *Kusinara* narrated these tales.
6(i) (ii)	*Sanjiva Jataka* *Samkhipta Jataka*	150 530	After *Devadatta* was swallowed by the earth, *Ajatasatru* got extremely frightened expecting a similar fate for himself. He came to the Lord with *Jivaka*. On this occasion, the Lord narrated the tale.
7(i) (ii)	*Kalayamusthi Jataka* *Kosiya Jataka*	176 226	The king of *Kosala* had set out for an armed expedition to put down a rebellion in the monsoon. When he came to Lord *Buddha*, he

Sl.No.	Title	Jātaka No.	Short Commentary
			prevented the King's untimely expedition by narrating these tales.
8(i) (ii) (iii) (iv) (v)	*Mahapingala Jataka* *Kapi Jataka* *Chedi Jataka* *Dharma Jataka* *Amra Jātaka*	240 404 422 457 474	*Devadatta*, the devil was swallowed by the earth, which was cheered by all the living creatures. *Buddha* narrated these tales on this occasion.
9	*Sujata Jataka*	269	*Sujata*, the daughter-in-law of King *Anatha-pindika* behaved in a rude manner with everyone at her in-laws' house. The Lord changed her by telling this tale.
10	*Vardaki-Sukara Jataka*	283	King *Prasenjit* was beaten by *Ajatasatru* in wars many a times. Ultimately *Prasenjit* defeated *Ajatasatru* by fighting as per strategy taught by Elder *Dhanugrahatissa*. This tale was narrated on this occasion.
11(i) (ii)	*Nana-chhanda Jataka* *Jyotsna Jataka*	289 456	Elder *Ananda* got eight boons from the blessed one. The tale is narrated on that occasion.

Sl.No.	Title	Jātaka No.	Short Commentary
12(i) (ii)	*Sujata Jataka* *Bhallatika Jataka*	306 504	King *Prasenjit* and Queen *Mallika* quarrelled on conjugal rights. The Master set this right by narrating these tales.
13(i) (ii)	*Tusa Jataka* *Musika Jataka*	338 373	By narrating these tales to King *Bimbisara*, when, *Ajatasatru* was a child, *Buddha* warned him that his son may kill him in future to capture the throne forcibly.
14	*Kosambi Jataka*	428	Once the Brotherhood dwelling at *Ghosita* Park near *Kosambi* stirred up a quarrel over a petty matter. To reconcile them, the Enlightened One narrated this tale in vain.
15	*Maha-dharmapala*	447	This tale was narrated to King *Suddhodana* by *Buddha* when he returned to Kapilapura after attaining Buddhahood.
16	*Bhadrasala Jataka*	465	*Virhurava*, the king of *Kosala* wanted to slain all *Sakyas*. The lord saved them thrice but failed in the 4th time. The tale followed the massacar.

Sl.No.	Title	Jātaka No.	Short Commentary
17	*Ruru Jataka*	482	The Blessed one told this tale to the ungrateful *Devadatta.*
18	*Sarava-mriga Jataka*	483	To anchor the peoples' faith on the truth rather than on the false ascetics, the Lord performed a miracle followed by this tale.
19	*Chandra-kinnara* Jataka	485	The Master went to *Kapilapura* after attaining Buddhahood and narrated this to his wife *Yashodhara.*
20(i) (ii)	*Saktigulma Jataka* *Mahakapi Jataka*	503 516	*Devadatta* threw a stone to kill the Master. A fragment only pierced his foot. *Jivaka* cured him. The tales follwed the incident.
21	*Sarabhanga Jataka*	522	This tale was narrated by the master after the death of Elder *Moggaliana.*
22	*Chullahamsa Jataka*	533	*Devadatta* arranged to let loose an infuriated Elephant named *Nalagiri* to kill *Tathagata.* The Elephant, instead of attacking, bowed before the Lord in esteem. This tale followed the Incident.

Sl.No.	Title	Jātaka No.	Short Commentary
23	*Khandahala Jataka*	542	*Devadatta* deployed a group of Archers to kill *Buddha*. But they failed to kill him and fell to his feet. Thereupon followed the tale
24.	*Mahanarada kassapa*	544	The Blessed One, along with *Uruvela Kassapa*, went to meet King *Bimbisara* after enlightenment as promised earlier. The tale followed the meet.
25	*Vissamvara Jataka*	547	After attaining Buddhahood the lord went to *Kapilapura*, when his elders showed reluctance to bow before him. He performed some miracles and the elders showed respect to him. Thereupon this tale was narrated by the Blessed One.

8.0 SELECT BIBLIOGRAPHY

SL. NO.	TITLE (LANGUAGE)	AUTHOR / EDITOR
1.	2500 Years of Buddhism (Eng.)	P V Bapat
2.	A Study on the Jātakas and the Avadānas (Eng.)	S C Sarkar
3.	Abhidharmattha Samgraha (Bng.)	S R Barua
4.	Aesop's Fables (Eng.)	Aesop
5.	Amitāva Buddha (Bng.)	A K Saha
6.	Analytical Study of Abhidhammakośa (Eng.)	Sukomal Chaudhury
7.	An Introduction to Abhidhamma (Eng.)	Silananda Brahmachari
8.	Arya Aṭṭhāṅgika Magga (Bng.)	B L Barua
9.	Atharva-veda Samhitā (Bng.)	B B Goswami
10.	Basic Buddhism Course (E)	Phra Sunthorn
11.	Bhasar Itibritta (Bng.)	Sukumar Sen
12.	Boudhya Sahitya o Sikkha Dikkhar Ruparekha (Bng.)	A C Banerjee
13.	Brahma-net Sutra (Eng.)	Sutra Transmission Committee of the US & Canada
14.	Buddha Dharmer Itihas (Bng.)	Manikuntala Halder
15.	Buddhist India	Rhys Davids
16.	Buddha Sahitya (Bng.)	B N Chaudhury
17.	Buddhism for Human Life (Eng.)	K Sri Dhammananda
18.	Buddhism in India and Abroad (Eng.)	A C Banerjee

SL. NO.	TITLE (LANGUAGE)	AUTHOR / EDITOR
19.	Chicago Speech (Eng.)	Swami Vivekananda
20.	Dream Symbolism in Śramanic Tradition (Eng.)	Jagadish P Sharma & Lee Siegel
21.	Ek Sahasra ek Arabya Rajani (Bng)	Tirthapati Dutta
22.	Facets of Early Buddhism (Eng.)	Bela Bhattacharya
23.	Folk Tales of Bengal (Eng.)	Lal Behari Dey
24.	Fundamentals of Buddhism (Eng.)	Peter D Santino
25.	Hindu Colonies in the Far East (Eng.)	R C Majumdar
26.	Hindu Gods and Goddesses (Eng.)	Swami Nirmalananda
27.	History of Buddhism (Eng.)	Manikuntala Halder
28.	Jātaka Manjarī (Bng.)	Ishan Ch. Ghosh
29.	Jātaka Nidāna (Bng.)	Dharmapāla
30.	Jātakatthavannanā (Pāli)	Fousböll
31.	Jātake Rāmkathā O Bhāratkathār Swarup Sandhān (Bng.)	Asha Das
32.	Jataker Patabhumikay Bangla Loka Sahitya (Bng.)	Asha Das
33.	Kathāsarit-Sāgara	Kamal Krishna Smritithirtha
34.	Mahābhārata (Bng.)	Vedavyās (Tr. K P Sinha)
35.	Mahābhārata (Bng.)	S R Ghosh
36.	Mahāmānav Gautama Buddha (Bng)	Sukomal Chaudhury
37.	Oupanisad (Bng.)	Chitrita Devi
38.	Prithibir Pauranik Kahini (Bng.)	Samabaya Publishers

SL. NO.	TITLE (LANGUAGE)	AUTHOR / EDITOR
39.	Political History of Ancient India (E)	Hemchandra Roychaudhury
40.	Pure-Land Zen, Zen Pure-Land (E)	Thick Thien Tam
41.	Pure Land, Pure Mind (E)	Chu-Hung & Tsung-Pen
42.	Pure Land of the Patriarch (E)	Han-Shan Te-Ching
43.	Ramayana (Bng.)	Hemchandra Bhattacharya
44.	Ratnamālā (Bng.)	Corp. body of the Buddha Edn. Fdn.
45.	Rik Veda Samhita (Bng.)	Ramesh Ch. Dutta
46.	Sama-veda Samhita (Bng.)	B B Goswami
47.	Sanskrita Sahityera Itihas (Bng.)	Gaurinath Sastri
48.	Srimat Bhagabat (Bng.)	Tarakanta Kavyatirtha
49.	Sri Sri Ramakrishna Kathamrita	As told by Srima
50.	Srimat Bhagavad Gita as it is (B)	Swami Prabhupada
51.	Stories from Panchatantra (Eng.)	Shivkumar
52.	Studies in Chinese Buddhism (Eng)	A C Banerjee
53.	Studies in the Buddhist Jātakas (E)	Binay Ch. Sen
54.	The Essence of Buddhism (Eng.)	P Laxmi Narasu
55.	The Dhammapada (Bng.)	Dharmadhar Mahasthabir
56.	The Four Buddhist Books in Mahayana	Upasika Chihmann (Ms. P C Lee)

SL. NO.	TITLE (LANGUAGE)	AUTHOR / EDITOR
57.	The Hitopadesa (Eng.)	G L Chandiramani
58.	The Jātaka (Eng.)	E B Cowell (2 Vols.)
59.	The Jātakas (Bng.)	Ishan Ch. Ghosh
60.	The Odyssey (Eng.)	Homer (Penguin)
61.	The path to reach (Eng.)	Ajahn Chah
62.	The Wings to Awakening (E)	Thanissaro Bhikkhu
63.	Valmiki Ramayana (Bng.)	Tarakanta Kavyatirtha
64.	Yajurveda Samhita	B B Goswami
	Lexicography	
65.	Bangla Bhasar Abhidhan	Samsad
66.	Bengali - English Dictionary	Samsad
67.	English Dictionary	Oxford
68.	English - Bengali Dictionary	Samsad
69.	Concise Pāli - English Dictionary	Aggamahā Pandita A P Buddhadatta Mahāthera
70.	Vidyarthi Bangla Abhidhan	Akademi

9.0 LIST OF ILLUSTRATIONS

9 List of Illustrations